19	5	IO	J	ZI
FELLER	BOUDREAU	HARDER	AVERILL	LEMON

25	14	20	42	455
THOME	DOBY	ROBINSON	ROBINSON	THE FANS

Career Numbers

The story behind the retired
numbers of the Cleveland Indians

By: Nicholas Brigeman

outskirts
press

Outskirts Press, Inc.
http://www.outskirtspress.com

ISBN: 978-1-9772-3647-0

Outskirts Press and the "OP" logo are trademarks belonging to Outskirts Press, Inc.

PRINTED IN THE UNITED STATES OF AMERICA

Table of Contents

Enjoy the book!

Go TRIBE!

_BH_

Foreword

By Vince McKee

WHAT'S IN A number? A lot! When I was asked by Nick to weigh in on this incredible scribe down Indians numerical history, I simply couldn't resist!

This story is so much more than just numbers, it has everything a diehard Indian's fan needs to know! This book gives in depth detail of the players Hall of Fame careers and the path that got them into the league. Where they grew up, their life before baseball and how they got started with the Tribe.

This book goes beyond the career statistics that earned the players baseball immortality. The reader will learn how several players responded when their number was called on and off the field.

Great players like Bob Feller who struck out 15 batters in his first Major League start but when the country needed him most in WWII, he chose freedom over fame. These are just some of the moments that this book will bring you.

I grew up always wanting to be 25, 55 or 13. Why you ask? Well it should be obvious, Jim Thome, Orel Hershiser and Omar Vizquel of course! A jersey number is so important to a child growing up playing sports, it is their first real shot at becoming an individual. Why not pattern it after one of your heroes'?

Perhaps most important is this little nugget, always remember, the team name can change, the logo can change, but that legendary number never will.

Enjoy this book, enjoy this amazing story, and most of all, enjoy being an Indian's fan!

Vince McKee

9x Published Author

Founder and CEO of Kee On Sports Media Group

@sports_kee

Introduction

GENERATIONS OF CLEVELAND baseball fans, when entering the home of the Indians gaze at upper deck corner of right field and see the names and numbers of immortalized Cleveland Indians greats:

Feller, 19
Boudreau, 5
Averill, 3
Lemon, 21
Thome, 25
Doby, 14.
Robinson, 20
Robinson, 42
Harder, 18
and
The Fans 455

Some baseball players wore the same number as many other players; Babe Ruth and Earl Averill both wore the number 3. Most players made their debut with a number on their back, but only a handful of players have made the number that they wore immortal. Since the early days of the game several players have been remembered for their outstanding careers by having their numbers retired, and members of the Cleveland Indians are no exception.

In 1916 the Cleveland Indians became the first team to have players wear numbers on their uniforms when they debuted with roman numerals on their sleeves. The league did not approve of the look however, so Cleveland was asked to remove the numbers. By 1929 the New York Yankees had plans to start the season with numbers on their backs. Mother nature intervened and caused New York to postpone the team's opening day so the Cleveland Indians became the first team in the majors to regularly wear numbers on the back of their uniforms.

Since the inception of the Cleveland baseball teams in 1901, nearly 2,000 players have donned the uniform for the American League Club [1]. Progressive Field is where the Indians currently play their home games, and the Cleveland Indians organization has permanently retired eight player's numbers, prominently displaying the legend's name and jersey number in the rafters in right-field. These numbers have been on display for generations of fans; old timers who may have witnessed the players dominance, and young fans who only see display as a name and number. But these players are also members of Cooperstown, Major League Baseball's Hall of Fame. The Indians have a franchise rule that a player's number can only be retired once they are inducted into the Hall of Fame.

For nearly a century, millions of fans across the country were in the presence of some of baseball's greatest players. For the Indians, four of these famous players won a World Series while another had the distinction of playing in two World Series matchups. These players showed off their talents to some of the hardiest fans in the game, and more retired numbers are sure to follow. This book gives an overview of the stories behind the names and jersey numbers immortalized in Cleveland Indians history; their accomplishments on and off the field and the facts that tell the narrative of their inspiring play. In addition to those who played on the field for the Indians, there are two numbers of enduring fame also displayed for all fans to see. Read on to understand more about the legends of the game of Cleveland Indian's Baseball.

CHAPTER 1

MEL 18 HARDER

(Born October 15,1909 Died October 20, 2002)

BORN ON HIS family's farm in Beemer, Nebraska young Mel was athletic, but his nearsightedness kept him from playing many sports. When he was just 2-years old his family moved to Omaha where he grew up and began to learn the game of baseball in his early school years. Using homemade equipment, Mel mostly played ball during recess and on the weekends with his friends. By the age of 10 he had joined a church league where he played the positions of both centerfielder and pitcher. It was then Mel started to develop his pitching skills. He learned to pitch a quality fastball and a sinker, but his famous curveball was not part of his repertoire until he reached the Majors.

As a teenager Mel attended Omaha Tech High School and by the age of 17, he could change speeds and spot the ball's location well enough to throw off the timing of the batters he faced. As a sophomore in high school his team won the state title and Mel was offered a minor-league contract from the Omaha Buffaloes. Mel started the 1927 season with the Buffaloes but was not given the opportunity to pitch in any games. Instead, he was sent down to the class D

Mississippi Valley League to pitch for the Dubuque Dubs where he had a record of 13-6. Mel's record helped build his team's lead in the standings and his success grew to the point where Major League clubs started to take notice. Before he was good enough to play in the Majors, Mel had to hone his craft with the Buffaloes and his Major League career had to wait.

While facing tougher competition, Mel won 4 games in 11 appearances and three professional teams including the St. Louis Cardinals, Chicago White Sox and the Cleveland Indians took interest in signing him. Mel played with the Omaha Buffaloes for nearly three-months and his contract was sold to Cleveland for $6,750. The Indians general manager Cy Slapnicka had seen him pitch in the minors and was impressed with his arm, and Mel signed with the Indians before the start of the 1928 season.

During spring training in 1928 Mel was one of the few teenagers who had a realistic chance of making the opening day roster and he did just that. His play stood out with his ability to fool batters with a sinking fastball and his opponents were often left swinging at air. When batters did make contact, often the ball would be grounded into the dirt and the fielders would throw the batter out. His outstanding control helped him to walk few batters and rarely surrender the long ball. The 18-year old was the youngest player in the Majors that season and he spent most of his rookie year eating up innings as a reliever. Learning from his teammates, George Uhle and Willis Hudlin, Mel's curveball began to take shape.

His Major League debut came on April 24, 1928 when he pitched 3 2/3 scoreless innings of relief against the St. Louis Browns at Sportsman's Park in St. Louis. Although his first big league game was one of his best, Mel struggled his rookie year and was kept in the bullpen. His first career start came on September 27, 1928 in game 2 of a doubleheader against Boston. Mel surrendered 10 hits in seven complete innings and the Red Sox handed him his second loss of the season. Mel finished his rookie campaign making 23 appearances, pitching 49 total innings with a record of 0-2 and an ERA of 6.61.

Midway through the 1929 season Mel continued with his pitching woes as a reliever. In June, the team sent him to the minors to eat up innings and get more experience with the New Orleans Pelicans where he went 7-2 in 16 starts. His pitching improved and come September he was called up and made one last appearance on the season. Trailing against the White Sox, the Tribe rallied for three-runs in the ninth inning to snatch a 9-7 victory giving Mel his first career Major League win.

By the time his third season began in 1930, Mel had worked his way into the starting rotation. The Indians used him as a swingman pitcher allowing him to pitch both as a starter and reliever. Making 19 starts and pitching 17 games in relief, Harder finished with an 11-10 record and a 4.21 ERA. The rising star also pitched seven complete games. Mel racked up 45 strikeouts in 175 1/3 innings of work and continued the same role in 1931.

At the start of his fifth season in 1932, Mel had permanently become a starter and it was the beginning of some of his best seasons with Cleveland. On the last day of July 1932, Mel had the honor of starting the first ballgame at Municipal Stadium, Cleveland's brand-new ballpark. The park was packed with 80,000 plus screaming fans, by far the largest crowd in those days. The Indians battled but came up short losing 1-0 to the Philadelphia Athletics. The difference was a ground ball hit by Mickey Cochrane in the eighth inning that got beyond the reach of Mel's glove.

3

In 1934, Mel had one of his best seasons developing a nasty curveball and finishing with a low ERA of 2.61, second best in the league. Along with his outstanding ERA, Mel had an impressive 20-12 record. He led the American League in shutouts with six and ranked sixteenth in MVP voting. His standout numbers earned him a spot on the American League All-Star roster, his first of four consecutive appearances.

On the afternoon of July 10[th,] 1934 at the Polo Grounds Park, New York hosted baseball's All-Star Game. The American League All-Stars faced the National League All-Stars in what is commonly referred to as baseball's Mid-Summer Classic. This was just the second All-Star game in Major League baseball history and Indians pitcher Mel Harder played a big role. In the fifth inning, American League pitcher Red Ruffing had issues getting batters out allowing four men to reach base and two runs to score. Mel was called on to get the team out of the jam, and with runners on first and second with nobody out he had his work cut out for him. Future Hall of Famer Mel Ott lined the base-ball into the outfield but a force-out at second was the first out in the inning. The next man for Mel to face was Paul Waner of the Pittsburgh Pirates, another future Hall of Famer. The batter struck out on a curve-ball in the dirt and Mel needed one more out. He allowed a walk, but Mel and the American League All-Stars retired Arky Vaughan, an-other future Hall of Famer, on a fielder's choice. The National League scored on a double steal while Mel was on the mound, but all three runs were charged against Red Ruffing. Clinging to an 8-7 lead, Mel stayed in the game pitching a full 5 innings and gave up no runs. He faced 18 batters, 14 of them future Hall of Famers. He only surren-dered a single hit, a walk, and he fanned two batters. He is the only American League pitcher to pitch five shutout innings in an All-Star game. The American-League won the game 9-7 and with his standout numbers he was the pitcher of record and earned the win.

In 1935 Mel continued his brilliance on the mound, posting a career best 22 wins and finishing in the top 30 of Most Valuable Player voting. He led the league with the fewest walks with 1.7 walks per nine innings and only 0.2 home runs per nine innings. At that point in his career he was considered the Indians ace and even the best hitters struggled against him. In his 35 starts, Harder struck out 95 batters while only walking 53 in 287 1/3 innings pitched.

That same season on July 8, the Cleveland Indians were selected to be the franchise to host the All-Star Game at Municipal Stadium. The Mid-Summer Classic exhibition game set an attendance record with 69,812 fans in the ballpark, a record that stood until 1981 when 72,000 fans attended the All-Star game at the same ballpark. For the second straight season, the Indians ace pitched in relief, allowing no earned runs in 3 innings of work. The American League All-Stars won the ballgame 4-1 and Mel was credited with the save. His All-Star numbers over the past two seasons were a strong 1-0, in eight innings of work allowing no runs on just two hits. With this new tradition, The American League All-Stars had won the first three matchups ever with Mel Harder on the winning side twice.

Later that month on July 31, Harder had a rough outing against the Chicago White Sox. He surrendered 12 hits, all 6 runs and the Tribe was on the losing end of a 6-4 score. The pitcher did however show off his power by hitting two solo home runs both coming against Chicago's starter Ray Phelps. The Indians and the White Sox have always been part of the American-League but back then, every pitcher was required to bat. This rule was part of the league until January 11,1973 when owners of the 24 teams took a vote to allow a designated hitter to bat while keeping the same pitcher in the game.

During the 1936 season, when he was just 26 years-old, Mel was not off to the greatest of starts. He did however continue to flourish in his third straight All-Star appearance, pitching two more scoreless innings while only allowing 2 hits. The final score of the game was 4-3 with the National League earning their first All-Star-Game victory since its debut back in 1933, but Mel was not credited with the loss. In just his second start after the break, the Indian's ace was feeling pain in his shoulder, but he managed to pitch through the pain and win two straight games. His next four starts were painful physically and statistically. Over a combined 23 innings, Mel's ERA was an awful 11.35 winning just one game. He decided to ride the bench for twelve days but when he returned, he was not the same dominant pitcher as before. In six starts and two relief appearances Mel ate up 34 1/3 total innings, but his ERA climbed above 5 to close out the season. In 1936 Harder was a .500 pitcher 15-15 in 36 games. His injury was a big blow for Cleveland as they were in a race for the division title, but they did not have the pitching to overcome the White Sox.

Mel spent time in the off season building up his arm strength again and by spring he was ready to start fresh. However, his years of dominance were over. That July 1937 Harder pitched in relief for a fourth straight All-Star Game and again he surrendered zero runs. Harder's All-Star numbers are an impressive 1-0 record with 2 saves, in 13 innings pitched. He allowed just 9 hits and 0 earned runs. He is the only pitcher to pitch ten or more scoreless innings his entire All-Star career.

Mel Harder played his entire 20- year career with the Indians from 1928-1947. He spent more seasons in Cleveland than any player in franchise history. Harder unfortunately retired in 1947, one year prior to Cleveland winning just their second World Series title ever. Although he was no longer a player, he was the team's pitching coach when the Indians beat the Boston Braves 4 games to 2 in the Fall Classic the following season. During his 16 seasons as the Tribe's pitching coach, he helped develop several of baseball's greatest hurlers in Bob Lemon, Early Wynn, and Bob Feller.

Harder would later coach with the New York Mets, Chicago Cubs, Cincinnati Reds, and Kansas City Royals, and is regarded not only as one of Major League Baseball's all time best pitchers, but also as one of the best pitching coaches of all time.

The Cleveland Indians have 8 retired numbers and a team rule that a player can only have their number retired if they are in Cooperstown, baseball's Hall of Fame. Mel Harder is one of the eight players to have a jersey number retired but he is not in baseball's Hall of Fame. An exception was made however, he played for 20 seasons with the Indians and spent more than fifteen seasons as the team's pitching coach. The Cleveland Indians retired Melvin Leroy Harder's number (18) in 1990.

MEL HARDER'S CAREER NUMBERS.

223 Wins 186 Losses .545 Win Percentage 3.80 ERA 1,161 Strikeouts 3,426 1/3 Innings Pitched

CAREER HIGHLIGHTS

1. In 1933 Mel Harder pitched a total of 253 innings and Led the American League with a 2.95 ERA.

2. Cleveland Municipal Stadium opened on July 31, 1932. The Indians played the Philadelphia Athletics in front of a sellout crowd of 80,142 fans. Mel Harder was given the honor of pitching the very first game at the new ballpark.

3. On July 14, 1934 Mel Harder out pitched Washington's starting pitcher Earl Whitehill throwing a complete game 2-0 shutout while surrendering only four hits. The Indians defeated baseball's defending American-League champions.

4. The same season on September 2, Mel and the Tribe battled and blanked their rivals the Tigers winning by the slimmest of margins 1-0. Harder struck out 3 Tiger batters in 9 innings.

5. 1934 was one of his best seasons. Mel Harder won 20 games while pitching a total 255 1/3 innings and posting an ERA of 2.61. He led the AL in shutouts that season with 6.

6. During the 1935 season on April 16, Harder pitched a career high fourteen innings in one game while leading the Indians to a 2-1 victory against the St. Louis Browns. Harder allowed 8 hits and struck out 6.

7. On September 20, 1942 Mel Harder pitched in game two of a doubleheader against the Tigers. Mel allowed 6 walks but gave up no runs and led the Indians to a 2-0 complete game shutout after the Tribe lost in game one 6-5.

8. Between 1934-1937 Mel Harder was a four time All-Star. Mel was credited with a victory in his first appearance pitching 5 shutout innings. He finished his All-Star career with 1 win 0 losses and 2 saves in 13 innings pitched. Harder never allowed a run or an earned run to come home. One of his two saves came in front of the home crowd at Cleveland Municipal Stadium.

CHAPTER 2

EARL 3 AVERILL

(Born May 21, 1902 Died August 16, 1983)

MAJOR LEAGUE BASEBALL has consistently been able to produce stars and Howard Earl Averill is one of them. Born in the small town of Snohomish, Washington, as a child Howard loved to play ball. Long before he made baseball his passion, he suffered the loss of two family members. His father Jotham died from pneumonia when he was just two years old. Six years later his older brother Easter died as well.

When he was growing up, often Howard played baseball with friends in a field that was cleared of rocks and tree stumps by the townspeople. The equipment he played with was homemade since most balls, bats, and gloves were unaffordable for he and his friends. For reasons unknown from his early days of playing the game and for his entire career Howard went by his middle name Earl. No matter the reason, Earl played with his friends every chance he had. He was gifted at baseball and worked hard at getting better almost every day. Earl mostly practiced as an outfielder, practicing his accuracy and catching techniques, but one day when he was 15, he felt pain in his arm, and he was unable to throw a baseball. The pain in his shoulder, known then as dead arm, was likely caused from constantly throwing the ball hard and often.

Since he was living with a single parent, Earl was forced to quit school and the game he loved to help support his family. One of his many jobs was working at a greenhouse that his older brother Forrest owned. Growing flowers at the greenhouse became a second passion for him during his time away from the game. The young teenager worked hard for his family, but that did not keep him from playing ball and trying to turn it into a Big-League career. For Earl baseball was life and he was good at it. In 1920 a local team called the Pilchuckers was founded and Earl was invited to the tryouts. The team name came from the Pilchuck River located in Snohomish where he grew up. This was the start of his semi-pro career as he played with that team for several seasons.

By the age of 19 in 1922, Earl married Loette Hyatt. They had four sons and stayed married for the rest of their lives. Local townspeople liked what they saw from Earl's game and many people genuinely believed he could play baseball at the Major League level. In 1924 people that knew of his talent paid his way to try out for the Seattle Indians team in San Bernadino, California. To his misfortune, he was told he was not good enough to play for the Pacific Coast League and was sent home. Disappointed by the outcome, it still was not enough to make Earl give up.

Back home in Washington, the Bellingham local team found him work and offered him a tryout. The team was not blown away by his performance as he batted below .300 but they let him hang around for the 1925 season. During his second season with Bellingham, his bat exploded with an average that climbed above .400. His increased batting average caught the attention of the San Francisco Seals, a team from the same league that told him he was not good enough to play baseball. Playing in his first season, his average stayed near the .400 mark and he helped lead the last place Seals to one game out of first place.

The Seals invited him back for spring training in 1926 where he signed a contract and by his third season in 1928, his team won the Pacific Coast Championship. That year he led the league with 173 runs scored and a .354 batting average. Now it was clear, Earl had Major League talent. After the season had ended, San Francisco sold Earl's contract to the Cleveland Indians for what was reported to be a staggering $50,000. The man who was told he would not be able to play baseball was now playing at the Big-League level.

Averill was nearly 27- years old when he made his Major League debut on opening day April 16, 1929. It was unusual to have a rookie start their career in their late twenties. Another concern was would he be big enough to play? When the Indians owner first met Earl, he responded by saying, "you paid all that money for a midget?"[2] Stepping up to the plate for his first at-bat Earl faced Tigers hurler Earl Whitehill and the odds were against him. The rookie battled until he got a pitch to his liking and he hammered a home run! Averill had become only the second American League player to start his career with a round tripper. With one swing, the rookie had his first career hit, RBI, home run, and run scored. Cleveland fought hard to win the ballgame 5-4 in 11 innings. Despite never receiving any formal coaching or instruction, Earl Averill became one of the most promising and gifted players in the game. As Averill said, "Nobody ever taught me much of anything. You were on your own when it came to fundamentals." [3]

Averill quickly proved that he had the talent to perform at the Major League level. The 5'9" centerfielder became a line-drive machine and had one of the best rookie seasons for Cleveland in over a decade. He played the entire season collecting 198 hits. He drove in 96 RBI's, scored 110 times, and had an outstanding batting average of .332. To top it off, Earl set the team record smashing18 home runs, the most by a rookie.

Averill performed so well in his first season that his salary had been raised to $12,000 per year. The Indians manager Roger Peckinpaugh stated, "He's the best-looking youngster to come up in a long time."[4] With the amount of money spent on their new centerfielder, the Indians had themselves a bona fide star. During his second season playing for the Tribe his batting numbers increased in every category. Earl homered 19 times, drove home 119 runs and his average grew by seven points up to .339. One of Averill's standout moments of the 1930 season took place during a doubleheader at League Park in Cleveland on September 17, 1930. Despite splitting the two games against the Washington Senators Earl made noise with his bat as the first player in Major League history to launch 4 home runs in a doubleheader. Cleveland defeated Washington 13-7 in game one but dropped game two by a final of 6-4. He tallied a combined 11 RBI's, as well as a grand slam and inside the park 3-run homer.

The 1931 season proved to be the best season for the now sea-soned veteran. Earl posted a career high in-home runs with 32, 143 RBI's and he came home to score 140 times. With his explosive bat, Earl ranked 3rd best in-home runs and RBI's in the big leagues, finishing behind Lou Gehrig and Babe Ruth. The Red Sox feared his bat so much he was walked intentionally 5 times in one game. The Indians finished in fourth place at 78-76-1 and missed the postseason. In fact, the Indians never played in the playoffs with Earl on their team. The centerfielder's big numbers did however earn him fourth place in the American League MVP voting in 1931.

Two seasons later, on July 6, 1933 Major League Baseball played the first All-Star Game and Earl was invited to play. Two teams, the American League All-Stars (AL) and the National League All-Stars (NL) matched talents at Comiskey Park in Chicago, Illinois. In his fifth season, the Indians centerfielder played on the very first AL All-Star ballclub. Playing alongside some of baseball's greatest names in Lou Gehrig and Babe Ruth from the Yankees. During the contest, the great Bambino smashed a 2-run home run in the 3rd inning to give the American League a sizable 3-0 lead. By the time the 6th inning rolled around the American League lead was narrowed to 3-2. Earl Averill had been riding the bench but with the Senator's pitcher up to bat and an insurance run in scoring position he was called to the plate. Averill slapped a fastball into centerfield scoring the runner form second and increasing the American League lead by two runs. The score remained 4-2 and his RBI was arguably the biggest run in the game.

Later in 1933, nearly three-weeks into August and Cleveland's Earl Averill was making the headlines again. A Major League record 8 batters hit for the cycle during the 1933 season. Half of the players hit for the cycle in August, and all 4 of those contests involved an Athletics' batter or an opponent. On August 17, the Indians played host against the Philadelphia A's and Earl's bat took center stage. Philadelphia's pitcher George Earnshaw had his struggles, the pitcher's earned run average was above 5.80 for the season and it got worse from there. Averill doubled in the bottom of the first, hit a triple down the line in the third and came home to put the Tribe up 4-0 and remove Earnshaw from the game. The shutout was snapped in the top of the fifth inning when Philadelphia scored three times to cut the lead to 4-3. In the home half of the inning, the Tribe sent 13 batters to the plate and scored 7-runs one of them, an RBI single from Averill. In the home half of the seventh Averill batted needing a home run to complete the cycle. Cleveland was leading by 10-runs and he smashed a 2-run home run to increase the lead to 15-3. Averill had become just the second player in Cleveland franchise history to complete the cycle. Cleveland had won the game in convincing fashion 15-4 and Earl was in the record books.

Averill played in 6 consecutive All-Star games between 1933-1938. The one he is most remembered by came in the summer of 1937, and his play had a negative impact on the game. On the final play of the third inning, National League pitcher Dizzy Dean, who had won 133 games in his first five seasons, was struck by a line drive that hit him in his left toe. The batter was Earl Averill and Dean was sent to the showers. The All-Star pitcher Dean was never the same. Over the next three seasons he collected only 17 wins before he was forced to retire from baseball. Despite the unfortunate at-bat that took place during the Mid-Summer Classic, Earl's great moments outweighed the negative moments. His 11-year career as an outfielder with Cleveland were some of the greatest in franchise history.

The Cleveland Indians retired Howard Earl Averill's number (3) in 1975. Major League baseball inducted Averill into the Hall of Fame in 1975.

EARL AVERILL'S CAREER NUMBERS

6,353 At-Bats. 2,019 Hits. 1,224 Runs Scored. 238 Home Runs. 1,164 RBI's .318 Batting Average

CAREER HIGHILIGHTS

1. April 16, 1929 Major League debut Averill homered in his first Big-League at-bat. Cleveland won the game 5-4 against the Detroit Tigers.

2. In 1932, Averill led the American League centerfielders in assists with 11. Eight of the assists were double plays.

3. In his best season in 1931, Earl had a career high 32 home runs, 143 RBI's and ranked 4th overall in AL MVP voting.

4. During each of his first six seasons, Averill had a batting average above .300. His best came in his 2nd season in 1930 when he batted .339.

5. In his rookie season Earl set the team record for home runs with 18.

6. On September 17, 1930 Averill became the first batter in Major League history to homer 4 times in a doubleheader. Three home runs in game one, one home run in game two verses the Washington Senators in Cleveland.

7. On July 6, 1933 Earl Averill hit a pinch-hit RBI single in the very first All-Star Game. The American League All-Stars defeated the National League All-Stars 4-2.

8. August 17, 1933 Earl hit for the cycle in Cleveland against the Athletics and helped lead the Tribe to a 15-4 win. He became just the second player in franchise history to hit a single, double, triple and home run in the same game.

CHAPTER 3

BOB 19 FELLER

(Born November 3, 1918 Died December 15, 2010)

THERE WERE TWO types of fields in the farming town of Van Meter, Iowa: a field of corn and a baseball field. Living on his father's farm was a boy by the name of Robert Feller, a boy who would become a legend not only in Van Meter, but in all of baseball. Bob Feller grew up living the life of a hard-working farmer, but he had the arm strength of a Major League pitcher. It never mattered to young Bobby that he spent his days working in the hot sun. He would harvest the corn, milk the cows, and clean the chicken coops. After a long day's work his father Bill rewarded him by playing a game of catch. In the 1920's no matter who you were or what lifestyle you lived; most boys embraced the chance of playing ball with their father. Since the early days of the game that is how most boys learned to throw a ball, chase down a fly and swing a bat. Bill Feller learned the game from his father, and he wanted to do the very same for his young son.

At age 12 in the summer of 1930 Bob worked with his father for days on the farm building their own baseball field. They cut down 20 plus trees, plowed the fields and made a pitcher's mound. Long before the movie, the father and son had their very own field of dreams.

They built bleachers with the leftover wood and invited everybody to play baseball with the young star. Bill Feller named their beloved ballpark Oakview Park and charged crowds thirty-five cents to watch the young pitching prodigy. Bob Feller used his blistering fastball to strikeout grown men in their thirties. He would surely be at the next level soon. In 1935, Feller had begun pitching for the Farmers Union Insurance team in Des Moines and the 17-year old helped win the championship as the star pitcher. With his fantastic stuff he pitched five no-hitters in 3 seasons. Cy Slapnicka, the Cleveland Indian's general manager, was scouting a local pitcher by the name of Claude Passeau. Before the GM found Claude, he arrived at the Feller Farm and discovered Bob Feller. After Slapnicka witnessed Feller hurl his impressive fastball, he forgot all about the original pitching prospect and offered the 17-year old a contract: $1 and an autographed baseball. When Feller had signed the contract, he was still in his senior year at Van Meter High School. He joined the team and completed school during the offseason.

Bob Feller's Major League debut came on July 19, 1936 when he faced the Washington Senators in a relief appearance. Cleveland was down big, so Feller was called to eat up a single inning where he walked two batters and struck out one. About a month had passed and Feller had made five more relief appearances. He had pitched well, and many batters were afraid of getting hit by his blistering fastball. The farm boy's fastball was like nothing anyone had seen before and on August 23, 1936 he made his first career start. This was a bold move made by the Indians by sending their 17-year old rookie to the mound. Before the rookie faced the St. Louis Browns, Denny Galehouse had begun to loosen up in the bullpen in case the moment was too big for Feller. But the Browns batters had no answer and the rookie struck out the first batter he faced. Feller racked up the strikeouts in bunches and after five innings he had struck out 10 batters. St.

Louis scored the first run in the top of the 6th inning with two doubles, but the Indians responded with three-runs that same inning to move in front. The Indians scored a fourth run in the 7th inning and Bob Feller pitched a complete game 4-1 victory with 15 strikeouts. The rookie was superb in his first win and after the game a Brown's player requested to take a photo with him and he accepted. Bob Feller commented on his performance saying, "I was afraid that my arm would tire along about the sixth or seventh inning, but it held up fine."[5] His 15-strikeout performance had set the record for most strikeouts by an American-League pitcher in their starting debut. The news of Feller's performance spread quickly. Dodgers pitcher Van Mungo said "That showing was just a tip-off. You've got to be a good pitcher to strikeout 15 Major League batters in one game. Whether you're 17 years old or 27."[5]

Bob Feller's next two starts were road games where he had to pitch at some of the most difficult ballparks. In Fenway Park in Boston he suffered his first loss as the Red Sox scored 5-runs in five innings before he was pulled from the game. Feller's second road game at Yankee Stadium was worse. He struck out the first batter then gave up a single, three walks and 5-runs all in the first inning. Feller again left the game early. After his struggles on the road it was recommended by the coaching staff that the young pitcher should add off-speed pitches to his arsenal.

Feller's fortunes turned around when he faced the Browns for a second time on Labor Day. His second game against St. Louis proved his first start was not a fluke. The 17-year old struck out 10 batters and he pitched a complete game in an Indian's 7-1 win.

That same month a September doubleheader between the Indians and the Athletics took place. Cleveland's Bob Feller took to the mound in game two and he put on a show. Using his new off-speed pitches, he issued 9 walks, but he fanned 17 batters. Cleveland swept the home doubleheader with a 5-4 victory in game 1, and Feller's mound performance helped led the Indians to a 5-2 victory in game 2. With that 17-strikeout win, Feller was in the record books as he tied the record for most strikeouts in a single game, matching pitcher Dizzy Dean in 1933. Defeating Philadelphia gave Feller his third career win.

Bob Feller made 14 appearances during his first season, pitching a full 62 innings he posted a 5-3 record. With his blazing fastball he struck out 76 batters and finished with a 3.34 ERA. The rookie's fastball earned him several nicknames: "Rapid Robert Feller", "Fireballer Feller", and "The Heater from Van Meter". His future with the Cleveland Indians was bright.

Late in his third season on October 2, 1938 Feller took the mound against the Detroit Tigers. Cleveland lost the contest 4-1 but Feller set a record for most strikeouts in a game with 18. No pitcher came close to tying that record until the late 1990's. Any batter that faced Bob Feller would require some luck to reach base with a hit. By the end of the 1938 season Feller had made 36 starts and finished the season with 17 wins and 11 losses. His walk totals climbed to 208 but his strikeout total led the Majors with 240.

After 3 years of playing Big-League baseball Bob Feller had a record of 31-21 with 466 strikeouts. His Earned Run Average was a solid 3.60. Feller had the numbers to pitch for the American League All Stars in the 1939 All-Star Game, but injuries cost him that opportunity.

Baseball's seventh annual All-Star Game took place on July 11, 1939 at Yankee Stadium in New York. The American League All Stars had won four of the first six contest and every year a new star seemed to shine. The American League All Stars had taken a 3-1 advantage into the sixth inning, and all 3-runs were driven home by a Yankee batter. The hometown fans had lots to cheer about but needed quality pitching to keep the narrow lead. The National League had a golden opportunity to tie or take the lead before the seventh. The man in their way was Rapid Robert Feller. The bases were loaded but on his first pitch to Arky Vaughan, the inning was over. A groundball double play held the National League All-Stars scoreless. Still on the mound in the top of the 9th, Bob Feller had retired eight of the ten batters he had faced allowing a hit and a walk. The final two batters for the National League Johnny Mize and Stan Hack were both strikeout victims to end the game, with a score of 3-1 the American League All-Stars clinched another Mid-Summer Classic victory. Cleveland Indian's pitcher Bob Feller pitched 3 2/3 total innings, surrendering 0-runs, 1 walk and a hit. His strikeout total was not spectacular, but the young man racked up 2 in the last frame and earned himself a save.

Bob Feller rarely struggled during his career especially while facing the St. Louis Browns. In late 1939, in his third full season the Indians were on the road in St. Louis playing the Browns. That afternoon the Indians lit up the scoreboard scoring 12-runs against the Brown's pitchers and Feller held St. Louis to a single run. Feller fanned 5 batters and became the youngest pitcher in modern Major League Baseball to recorded 20 or more wins in a season and finished the 1939 campaign with 24 wins. For the second consecutive season Feller led the Majors in strikeouts with 246, six more than he had in 1938. Feller also pitched 296 2/3 innings which led all of baseball.

He continued his strong play, and his best games were still ahead of him. The Cleveland Indians began their 1940 season at Comiskey Park in Chicago against the White Sox. Once in a blue moon a player will do something so great, you may never see it again. In the same decade Yankee outfielder Joe DiMaggio set a Major League record whit his famous 56-game hitting streak. Bob Feller on the other hand took the mound on April 16 and pitched a game that cemented his name forever. The Indians batted first as the visiting team always does and were held scoreless by Eddie Smith for three innings. Batting in the fourth inning, the Tribe cracked the scoreboard 1-0 with a single and a 2 out RBI triple by Rollie Hemsley. For the Pale Hose, after 3 frames Feller had surrendered 4 walks, struck out 5 and left 5 men stranded. The performance was not perfect with his walks and an error by Cleveland's defense, but Chicago's line up was kept without a hit. All nine men in the field for the Indian's made the play when the ball was hit their way. By the eighth inning, Feller blew his heater past Joe Kuhel for his eighth punchout and the inning was over. Back to work for the ninth inning, with the score still 1-0 in Cleveland's favor with a big donut in the hit column for the White Sox. Chicago batter Mike Kreevich led off with an infield pop fly to second base...1 out. Moose Solters failed to provide a hit swinging and grounding out to shortstop Lou Boudreau. One out away from making history was Bob Feller, the 21-year-old from Iowa. The winning run, Taffy Wright came to bat after a man reached base via a base on balls. But Feller's pitch was grounded to the second baseman who fielded it well and got his man running to first and Feller started opening day 1940 with a gem! His teammates crowded around him on the mound celebrating what was an opening day for the ages! Feller had notched Major League Baseball's 109th no-hitter to date, his first no hitter and the first and only no hitter recorded on opening day. The White Sox players left Comiskey Park that evening with the same batting average that they started with .000. The Indians finished the 1940 season 89-65-1 as Bob Feller and the Indians missed the postseason falling out of first place by a single game.

In 1941 the team had a disappointing season. The Tribe went 75-79-1 finishing twenty-six games behind the New York Yankees. As a team Cleveland took a step in the wrong direction, but their 22-year old star pitcher led the American League in several categories. Robert pitched in 44 games and made 40 starts and for the third straight year led the American League in wins with 25. It was also the fourth consecutive season he led Major League Baseball with 260 strikeouts.

Between 1936-1941 Bob Feller had some of the greatest pitching numbers in the history of the game. To this point in his career he had made 175 starts and pitched 1,446 innings with 1,233 strikeouts. With only six seasons under his belt, it seemed as if Feller might set many Major League records given his young age and the number of seasons ahead of him. But on December 7, 1941, as Bob Feller was driving to Chicago to discuss his next contract with the Indians, he heard the dreadful news; America was attacked. "I was driving from my home in Van Meter, Iowa, to Chicago to discuss my next contract with the Cleveland Indians, and I heard over the car radio that the Japanese had just bombed Pearl Harbor. I was angry as hell."[6] Right then and there one of the greatest Major League players of his generation made up his mind to give up his career and serve his country. Feller made it to Chicago where he told Indian's general manager Cy Slapnicka of his decision.

By December 9, 1941 "Rapid" Robert Feller had been sworn in to begin his physical training for the Navy. Feller originally began serving as a Chief Petty Officer and assisted men in need of physical training. He made a request to go into combat and was given the opportunity to serve on the USS Alabama where he served as a gun-captain on the ship. The men on the battleship bombarded beaches in the Pacific and assisted victims of amphibious assaults. He and his mates aboard the Alabama survived two enemy bombs that struck the ship, but with luck on his side and a victory secured for American, the Alabama never lost a man in combat. In March of 1945 after serving his country he was sent to Great Lakes Naval training center where he managed the baseball team. Five months later he rejoined the Indians and made 9 starts winning 5 games and losing 3.

On April 30, 1946 Feller and the Tribe traveled to Yankee Stadium where Feller earned his second win of the young season. More importantly, Rapid Robert pitched his second career no-hitter. The hurler blew away 11 Yankee batters and the Indians catcher Frankie Hayes homered in the ninth to score the game's lone run. Feller and his defense did the rest.

Two years later in 1948 the Indians and the Red Sox battled to crown a league champion. The Indians won a single elimination game 8-3 to advance to the World Series. Cleveland's win at Fenway Park stopped an all Boston World Series as they would be facing the Boston Braves of the National League. It had been a long stretch for both teams since they last played in a World Series; the Indians their last appearance came in 1920, the Braves it dated all the way back to 1914. In the first contest Bob Feller and Johnny Sain were locked in a scoreless pitcher's dule with Boston batting in the eighth inning. Feller surrendered a walk to the Braves catcher Bill Salkeld to begin the inning. Pinch runner Phil Masi replaced Salkeld to put more speed on the bases for the potential go ahead run. With 2 outs the Braves Tommy Holmes singled home the deciding run as Cleveland failed to score the entire game. Bob Feller lost game one and Cleveland fell behind in the series. In game two the Tribe responded with a victory to even the series as the Braves scored their only run against Bob Lemon in the first inning. The Indians had been shutout for the first three innings but cracked the scoreboard in the fourth. Lou Boudreau started the inning with a leadoff double and scored on a single to re-tie the game. With one out, Cleveland's Larry Doby smoked an RBI single to move out in front 2-1. The final tally was 4-1 and an even series was headed to Cleveland.

It was Game 4 of the World Series played in Cleveland and the Indians were in search of a 3-1 series lead. Cleveland won the ballgame not because of their hitting, but their pitching. Steve Gromek pitched a complete game for the Indians as he tallied 2 strikeouts and was given just enough run support. In the bottom of the 1st inning, the Tribe scored the first run when the shortstop Lou Boudreau doubled home the left fielder Dale Mitchell. The scoreboard changed again in Cleveland's favor when the Tribe's outfielder Larry Doby blasted a solo home run over the wall in right field. The score was 2-0 and Doby had become the first African American to hit a home run in the World Series. The Boston Braves took their swings in the top of the 7th and collected a home run from the left fielder Marv Rickert, but it was too little too late as that remained the final score. The Indians starter Steve Gromek earned the win while the Braves starting hurler Johnny Sain took the loss. Now Cleveland could win the series if they took the next home game.

For the fifth game of the series, the third game in Cleveland, the Tribe led 3 games to 1. Once again Boston had their way with Cleveland's ace Bob Feller. In 6 1/3 innings he allowed 3 home runs and the Boston Braves lived to play another day as they won 11-5, with seven runs allowed by Feller. The road victory sent the series back to Boston and the Indians captured the elusive fourth victory to win the World Series winning game six by a score of 4-3. Bob Lemon earned his second win of the series and for the first time since 1920 the Indians were World Champions! Although Feller was unable to claim a pitching victory, he was an integral member of what is still today the last World Series won by the Cleveland Indians.

The 1956 season was Bob Feller's last year in the Majors. Feller played his entire career with the Indians and what a career for the Heater from Van Meter. The Cleveland Indians retired Robert William

Andrew Feller's number (19) the very same year Major League Baseball Inducted Feller into the Hall of Fame in 1962. Without a doubt Bob Feller had a legendary career with the Cleveland Indians winning more than 260 games with thousands of strikeouts recorded and 3-no-hitters pitched. But you have to wonder what his final stats would show had he not left to serve his country. Feller very well could have recorded 3-more twenty-win seasons with 100 or more strike-outs each. Three baseball seasons is a lot to give up but knowing what was at stake he chose freedom over fame.

BOB FELLER'S CAREER NUMBERS.

266 Wins. 162 Losses. .621 Win Percentage 3.25 ERA. 2,581 Strikeouts. 3,827 Innings Pitched 3 No-Hitters

CAREER HIGHLIGHTS

1. Bob Feller led the AL in wins six times. In 1940 he collected his career high 27 wins and in 1946 Feller led the Majors in total strikeouts as he fanned 348 total batters.

2. Bob Feller's strikeout pitch was his fastball. When he made his first start in 1936, he fanned the first man he faced, with 15 total strikeouts and a win.

3. Given the nickname the 'Heater from Van Meter' and 'Rapid Robert Feller', Bob set an MLB record with 18K's in a game facing the Detroit Tigers. Very few pitchers have matched the record.

4. During the 1939 All-Star Game Bob Feller earned the save pitching 3 2/3 scoreless innings at Yankee Stadium.

5. On April 16, 1940, Bob Feller pitched an absolute gem at Comiskey Park in Chicago. Cleveland's ace fanned 8 batters and he pitched baseball's first and only no-hitter on opening day. Cleveland won the ballgame 1-0. It remains the only no-hitter thrown on opening day.

6. Bob Feller had 3 career no-hitters. One in 1940 vs the White Sox, the second in 1946 vs the Yankees, and the third in 1951 in Cleveland against the Tigers.

7. Bob Feller pitched 12 career 1-hitters. Had he collected a fourth or fifth no-hitter, the Cy-Young trophy could very well be named after him.

8. The true story of the Feller Farm is remarkably similar to the popular movie "Field of Dreams" released in 1989. A farmer form Iowa heard a voice telling him "If you build it, they will come." Like the fictional movie, Bill Feller (Bob's father) built a baseball field in Iowa and sold tickets to people who wanted to play with the young star. The most important man who came was Cy Slapnicka the Indians General Manager who signed Feller to the Indians when he was only 17-years old.

CHAPTER 4

LOU 5 BOUDREAU

(Born July 17, 1917 Died August 10, 2001)

BASKETBALL AND BASEBALL, two sports with vastly different identities. Basketball is an up-tempo game and time plays a factor. The game of baseball is intended to involve zero physicality, the pace is slower, and the game is ended after a number of 'outs' not by a ticking clock.

Born in Harvey, Illinois, Lou Boudreau grew up with his father Louis Boudreau Sr. and his mother Birdie Boudreau. He spent most of his childhood playing baseball and basketball and was highly skilled at both games. The only question was, what rout would he take? Lou's father knew of his son's love for basketball but wanted Lou Jr. to fulfill his dead dream of playing in the Majors.

Louis Sr. was once a semi-pro third basemen for a ball club in Kankakee, Illinois but never made it to the Majors. His vision was to have young Lou thrive at the Big-League level. He would often take Lou to the park and hit 100 groundballs to his son and counted his errors. Lou attended Thornton Township High School in his hometown of Harvey, Illinois a school with no baseball team. He showed off his athleticism becoming one of the best playmakers on the basketball team and racked up the assist. Between 1933-1935 Lou's team the Flying Clouds went to 3 straight championship games, winning the title in 1933 but finishing second in '34 and '35. Lou led the team in assist all three years and become the first player in the history of Illinois to compete for three straight basketball titles.

Playing both basketball and baseball in his college days at the University of Illinois, Boudreau flourished as the team captain for both sports. Playing for the Fighting Illini, he helped carry both teams to Big Ten Titles in 1937. During his sophomore year Boudreau batted .347 with 25 hits and 4 triples as a third basemen, and for the 1937-38 basketball season was named an All-American. He wore the number 5 for both sports and in 1992 the University of Illinois retired his baseball number. Only two other Fighting Illini legends have had their numbers retired, football stars Red Grange and Dick Butkus.

During his sophomore year Boudreau was offered three professional sports contracts. Given choices between the first year NBL (National Basketball League) and Major League Baseball's Chicago Cubs or the Cleveland Indians. Boudreau made the decision to play Professional Baseball for the Indians because General Manager Cy Slapnicka scouted him in college. He also remembered playing ball with his father and wanted to fill the void of his father's Major League dreams. His newly signed contract made him ineligible to play amateur sports his junior and senior years of college, ending his storied collegiate career. He did however play one year of professional basketball for the Hammond Cesar All-Americans of the NBL during his senior year of college before concentrating on baseball.

The Indians were patient with their new third basemen and had him play ball for the Class B Three-League team in the minors and in 1938 the near 21-year-old played in 60 games and batted 2.90. He was then called up to play for the Cleveland Indians, making his Major League debut on September 9, 1938 as a third baseman. During the game, with the Indians trailing, the skipper Ossie Vitt had him pinch-hit in the seventh inning in front of their home crowd. His two at bats were nothing more than a harmless groundout and a walk and the Tribe's newest member finished the game 0-1. His Major League debut came with 23-games remaining on the schedule and young Lou did not step into the batter's box again that season.

The winter of 1938 - '39 had come and gone for baseball and before long all teams were preparing for the start of the new 1939 season. Indians manager Ossie Vitt persuaded the young infielder to take on a new roll at shortstop since Ken Keltner had third base locked up. Boudreau started the year in New Orleans and adapted to his new position quickly learning from Greg Mulleavy the regular shortstop. The young infielder was taught well and in his 117 games in the minors he smoked 17 dingers, drove home 57-runs and batted an impressive .331. By August 7, 1939 Boudreau returned to the Big Leagues in Cleveland and finished the season with 19-RBI's and an average of .258 in 53 games.

Lou was now in the Majors as the Indians permanent shortstop - but unfortunately his father Lou Sr. passed away before his son returned to play. The 1940 season was Boudreau's first full season playing for the Cleveland Indians, a spot he held for the next 11 seasons. He became a crafty shortstop and helped turn 116 double plays his first full year. With his bat, he homered 9 times and drove in 101 RBI's. Lou Boudreau made the 1940 American League All-Star roster but had a quiet first outing. The National League scored 3-runs in the bottom of the first and the score stayed that way until the eighth inning. Boudreau came into the game in the bottom of the eighth with teammate Bob Feller on the mound. The young shortstop had zero balls hit his way and the game was over before he could grab a bat. The National League All-Stars blanked the American League 4-0 winning their third game in eight tries. The Cleveland Indians were kept from the playoffs finishing in second place behind the Tigers.

The following 1941 season the Tribe had a setback and by the time the annual Mid-Summer Classic arrived in 1941 the Indians were no longer contenders. Boudreau made it back to the All-Star Game however and this time he made his mark. He entered during the sixth inning at shortstop with his team leading the NL 1-0, but before he and his teammates recorded three outs, the scoreboard again showed a tie. For the first time in his career Lou grabbed a bat for the American League All-Stars, and in the bottom of the 6th the young infielder drove home Joe DiMaggio with a base hit to centerfield. With his 2 out knock, the American League had taken a 2-1 lead. The visiting NL All-Stars scored two more runs in the seventh to move in front 3-2. Boudreau prevented more damage as he stole a hit with an impressive barehanded grab at shortstop. A second at-bat for him resulted in another hit but no RBI. In the bottom of the 9th, the AL-All-Stars rallied 4 times to win the ballgame 7-5.

A great deal of drama and hype took place during the 1941 season. The excitement came not from the Indians but New York Yankee's centerfielder Joe DiMaggio. Beginning on May 15, 1941 DiMaggio began a hitting streak that lasted for more than two months. By July 1, his streak had reached 44 games which tied Willie Keeler's record. Game after game fans across the country focused on the Bronx batter, giving him the nicknames "Jolting Joe" or "Joe the One-Man Show". In each game DiMaggio recorded a hit after his 44th he set a record, and on the evening of July 17, 1941 he took his bat to Cleveland in search of number 57. A sellout crowd at Municipal Stadium stared down at home plate watching every at-bat closely. Twice DiMaggio was robbed of a hit by third basemen Ken Keltner. DiMaggio batted in the eighth inning in what likely would be his final chance to keep the streak alive as he faced the Indian's relief pitcher Jim Bagby Jr. DiMaggio smoked a hard grounder to shortstop Lou Boudreau who made a barehanded snare and his throw beat DiMaggio who lost the race to first base. The record hitting streak ended at 56 games, but the Cleveland crowd stood up and gave the hit machine a well-deserved standing ovation.

At the start of the 1942 season the Cleveland Indians promoted the team manager Roger Peckinpaugh to take over as general manager. Now the position of manager needed to be filled and the Indians shocked the league when they chose their young shortstop Lou Boudreau to both play the field and manage the team. The press, the fans, and his teammates were all against the idea of allowing the 24-year-old to play and manage. Boudreau had a lot to prove, the United States and Cleveland's ace Bob Feller had recently joined the war after Japan attacked Pearl Harbor and the Tribe's roster would have several new faces. One of the hardest decisions of Lou's new job was making the correct defensive alignments and at the right time. Lou Boudreau played in 147 games his first season as player-manager and the team fell to fourth place, 28-games behind the Yankees. He batted .283 and only drove home 58 runs with 2-home runs. His infield play was unusually poor as he committed twenty-six errors which led the American League. It did not take long for his fellow teammates to doubt his ability to both coach and play and demand he be replaced. Managing and playing any position was a tall task especially as a star infielder.

On July 14, 1946 Cleveland faced Boston and one of the hottest batters in their lineup was Ted Williams. The outfielder had the ability to hit the baseball to any open gap on the field. Boudreau devised a plan to keep him from hitting. During William's at-bats Boudreau signaled his infield to shift from their normal positions to either the left or right side of the infield. Ted smoked the ball into the glove of the Indian's defense, and it made Boudreau look like a genius. From that day forward the Indians and the league picked up on the strategy, now commonly used in many Major League games.

In 1947 as the season began Cleveland had not made it to the postseason under the leadership of player-manager Lou Boudreau. The team owner Bill Veeck had a chance to hire Casey Stengel as the new manager, but Boudreau's popularity grew over the years, so he allowed him to keep the job. During the 1947 season, the owner made the decision of signing Larry Doby to the Cleveland Indians. He signed with Cleveland as the first African American to play baseball in the American-League. Lou Boudreau introduced him to his team-mates and saying that they were opposed to the addition of Doby is putting it mildly. During the 1947 campaign Lou's average increased to .307 with 4 homers and 67 RBI's. In the field he turned 120 twin killers but in his sixth season as player-manager it was not enough to play postseason baseball.

The front office gave Boudreau one final chance in 1948 to make something happen with this club and that year not one, but two teams finished better than the Yankees. The Red Sox and the Indians both finished with a first-place tie and a single game was played to name the League Champion. On October 4 at Fenway Park the Tribe stole the road game winning by five-runs 8-3. Player-Manager Lou Boudreau hit a two out solo homerun in the first inning to move out in front early. The opposing pitcher was Denny Galehouse a former Indian before his days with the Red Sox. Later in the visiting half of the fifth with a 5-1 lead, Boudreau smoked another home run making the lead grand slam proof. Two dingers and two RBI's Boudreau's bat were a big reason why Cleveland made it to the World Series in 1948.

As a team, the Indians bats were silenced in the first game facing the Boston Braves of the 1948 World Series. Their ace Bob Feller fought hard but surrendered the only run late, and Lou Boudreau batted 4 times but collected no hits as the Indians fell behind early in the series. The second game at Braves Field the Tribe scored 4 times to re-tie the World Series at one game each. Lou Boudreau was one of 2 runners to score in the fourth to move ahead of Boston for good. The Series moved to Cleveland for the next three games and the Tribe took games 3 and 4 the Indians with a chance to win the World Series in front of a sellout Municipal Stadium crowd. However, the Boston Braves forced a game 6 with a road victory outplaying Boudreau's Indians 11-5. In the sixth game while facing Brave's pitcher Bill Voiselle in the top of the 3rd, Manager Lou Boudreau drove home the initial run to score outfielder Dale Mitchell. Cleveland led the game 1-0 with 21 outs to go. On defense Boudreau turned two double plays. One came in the third to end the inning and again in the Brave's half of the sixth. The Cleveland Indians won game 6 on the road after stopping a ninth inning rally and for the first time since 1920, the Indians had won the World Series!

Lou Boudreau played two more seasons with the Indians and retired in 1952 with the Red Sox. The Cleveland Indians retired Louis Boudreau Jr.'s number (5) in 1970. Major League Baseball inducted Boudreau into the Hall of Fame in 1970.

LOU BOUDREAU'S CAREER NUMBERS.

6,029 At-Bats. 1,779 Hits. 861 Runs Scored. 66 Home Runs.
789 RBI. .295 Batting Average

CAREER HIGHILIGHTS

1. Lou Boudreau's primary position with the Indians was playing short stop. Occasionally he played the role of backup catcher.

2. During the 1944 season Lou Boudreau led the Majors with 134 double plays turned.

3. During the 1941 All-Star Game Lou Boudreau hit an RBI single that scored baseball's best hitter, Joe DiMaggio.

4. Nine days later on July 17, 1941, in Cleveland, shortstop Lou Boudreau ended Joe DiMaggio's 56-Game hit streak. It was also Boudreau's 23rd Birthday.

5. At the start of the 1942 season Lou Boudreau was named the player-manager of the Indians.

6. On July 14, 1946 against the Red Sox manager Boudreau devised a new defensive strategy to defend Ted Williams who hit the ball to every part of the field. The third baseman, shortstop and second basemen were all shifted to where a pull hitter normally hit the ball, now a common strategy employed in the game. Baseball originally named the strategy the 'Boudreau Shift'.

7. Midway through the 1947 season Lou Boudreau and Bill

Veeck signed the first African American to the American League: outfielder Larry Doby

8. In 1948 Lou Boudreau coached his team to the World Series. Cleveland defeated the Boston Braves in 6 games and Boudreau became the first shortstop to win the MVP Award.

CHAPTER 5

BOB 21 LEMON

(Born September 22, 1920 - Died January 11, 2000)

BORN AND RAISED by his mother and father in San Bernardino, California Bob Lemon came from a family of avid baseball fans. At a young age Bob's father Earl moved the family to Long Beach where he was employed at an ice company. Earl also worked his own chicken farm. Earl Lemon worked hard to support his family and provide his son with the best baseball equipment available. It takes a lot of work to become a professional baseball player, and Bob practiced relentlessly with his father trying to master shortstop, third-base and the position of pitcher so he would be ready when given the chance. One day while practicing his curveball his lack of control caused him to hit his mother Ruth in the head.

During his senior year in 1938 he played shortstop at Woodrow Wilson High School where his baseball skills earned him the California state player of the year award. He also attracted the attention of several Major League teams when he was just 17. Although the Indians signed Bob Lemon as a pitcher, a lot would take place before he took the mound. During the 1938 season Lemon played in the minors with the Oswego Netherlands, a club affiliated with the

Canadian American League. The Indians pitching rotation was full and there was no room for him on the Major League team. Over the span of 123 games Lemon played in 75 but only pitched a single inning. Oswego tried Bob at both shortstop and the outfield and with his bat Lemon drove 7 balls over the wall. By the end of the season his average climbed above three hundred.

During the 1939 season he played for the New Orleans Pelicans and continued his role as a shortstop for two more seasons. Finally, in September of 1941 Bob Lemon was called up to join the Cleveland Indians. September 9, 1941 was Bob Lemon's debut; he entered the game at third-base with Cleveland in command 11-1, but his first Major League at-bat was put on hold with the game ending as Lemon stood in the on-deck circle. Three days later Lemon's first career hit came facing the Washington Senators and future pitching teammate Early Wynn. In the final days of his short Big-League season Lemon did not see much playing time and the Indians fell to fourth place with zero chance at making the postseason.

After spring training in 1942 Bob Lemon failed to make the Indian's Opening Day roster so he spent most of the season playing for the Minor League Baltimore Orioles. Playing mostly as a third baseman, the Orioles left-handed batter found his power stroke. Lemon homered 21 times, the most of his minor-league career. He flashed the leather turning 20 double plays and even assisted in a triple play on opening day.

Lemon's future looked promising but with the country at war, like many other players of his day, he put his career on hold and enlisted with the United States Navy. Since December of 1941, the United States had been at war. Baseball was known as the national pastime, a game that continued to be played during the war in the towns and ball parks across America, but also on the military bases by American soldiers and servicemen. Bob Lemon served at Los Alamitos Naval Air Station in California training for the Navy before he was sent to Hawaii. While in the Navy Lemon played ball with other players and prisoners of war, and played multiple positions including the outfield, third base and occasionally as a pitcher. Bob Lemon was a stand-out player for the 14th Naval Circuit in Hawaii, impressing both fans and other Major Leaguers who had also enlisted, and was 5th in the MVP voting for the league. At the time, Major League players played for their respective leagues and the American League defeated the National League in the Navy World Series, and on October 6, 1945 Bob Lemon pitched the winning game in front of 25,000 spectators. Lemon's teammates were convinced he could pitch well enough and urged him to become a full-time pitcher.

After the war, the Indians brought him back, but his position both with the team and in the field was still not set in stone. Ken Keltner had also returned with a contract extension and was the Tribe's key third baseman. Manager Lou Boudreau had gotten word of Lemon's pitching abilities but used him as an outfielder to start the 1946 season. Lemon could make plays in centerfield, but when it came to hitting, he was not producing at a high level. Pitchers blew him away and attacked him with Lemon's worst enemy, the changeup: "I could hit anything else they threw at me, but not the changeup, and the word got around pretty quick."[7]

Up to this point, the twenty-five-year-old spent his career in the minors or in the Navy, and in 1946 he appeared in 55 games but batted only .180 with only 1 home run. Do the Cleveland Indians even need him? But on June 3 the Indians played a road doubleheader against the Philadelphia Athletics and the below .500 Indians won the first game with Red Embree starting for the Tribe. It was game two when player-manager Lou Boudreau handed the baseball for Bob Lemon's first pitching start. His mound debut was no gem as he lasted just 3 2/3 innings and his team lost 3-2, but Lemon was given more chances to pitch, mostly as a reliever and with each appearance he showed more confidence and improvement. For the 1946 season the young pitcher made 5 starts and pitched 17 times in relief and finished with a record of 4-5 and posted his career best 2.49 ERA.

During the offseason, the Indians spoke with Lemon and convinced him to extend his contract as a full-time pitcher. Although his rookie deal had always listed him as a pitcher, Lemon wanted the same amount of playing time he got in the Minors. Cleveland had no room for him at third-base nor could he hit well enough for the Tribe to justify keeping his bat in the lineup. Lemon had two choices, sign as a pitcher or go back to the Minors. In the end Lemon agreed to the new contract when he learned he would be getting a raise. At the time, the Indians already had one of the most elite pitching staffs in baseball with Bob Feller and Gene Bearden in the rotation. Given the dominant starting rotation, Lemon started the 1947 season mostly pitching out of the bullpen, but it was in the bullpen where he learned techniques and how to pitch the curveball from his teammate Mel Harder. In 37 appearances and 15 starts Lemon's record was a successful 11-5 with an ERA of 3.44. With an earned run average below four, by that August Lemon became a starting pitcher for good, and for the remainder of the season tossed 6 complete games and a total of 167 1/3 innings.

The following season in 1948 Lemon pitched one of his best campaigns with a record of 20-14 in 37 starts. Lemon led the American League by pitching 20 complete games, including 10 shutouts and a league leading 293 2/3 innings pitched. On the final day of June, Lemon took to the mound and he hurled a no-hitter on the road against the Detroit Tigers. The Indians scored twice in their first at-bats and from there, Lemon stole the show. The once utility infielder fanned 4 Tigers and grabbed his eleventh win and became the ninth pitcher in Cleveland franchise history to pitch a no hitter. Lemon had notched a very impressive year for just his first full season as a starting pitcher. With the strength of the pitching staff Cleveland finished the regular season in first place with a 97-58 record, with Lemon and Bearden both recording 20 wins, and Bob Feller nearly matching their total with 19.

In the 1948 World Series Cleveland took on the Boston Braves, and Lemon and his teammates played the initial game on the road on October 6. In game 1 the Indians lost a nail biter by a final tally of 1-0. Bob Feller pitched a beauty but got no run support from his batters. Game 2 in Boston Bob Lemon was handed the baseball and he got the job done, the Braves got an early 1-run lead in the first on a base hit by Bob Elliot and from there the bats were silenced. Lemon pitched a complete game with 5 strikeouts and plenty of run support, winning the game 4-1 as the Indians re-tied the series thanks to Bob Lemon's gem. The Tribe took a 3-1 series lead with a chance to clinch their first title at home since 1920, but on October 10th Boston dominated the fifth game 11-5. Back in Boston, Cleveland once again sent star pitcher Bob Lemon to the mound in hopes of avoiding a game 7. Lemon delivered with 7 1/3 innings of strong pitching with 1 strikeout as Cleveland battled to win 4-3, for the second time ever they were World Champions! Winning a World Series takes a team effort but as an individual, Bob Lemon had his best stuff. His World Series record was 2-0 with two road wins. Lemon struck out 6 batters in 16 1/3 total innings.

Over the next decade Lemon became one of the League's top pitchers and played in 7 All-Star Games. Even the greatest pitchers have their slumps. In 1949 Lemon lost 4 in a row and was asked how he planned to get on track? He responded by saying, "I had bad days on the field. But I don't take them home with me. I left them in a bar along the way home."[8] Lemon's career with Cleveland ended in 1958. The Cleveland Indians retired Robert Granville Lemon's number (21) in 1998. Major League Baseball Inducted Lemon into the Hall of Fame in 1976.

BOB LEMON'S CAREER NUMBERS

207 Wins 128 Losses. .618 Win Percentage. 3.23 ERA
1,277 Strikeouts and 2,850 Innings pitched. 1 No-Hitter

CAREER HIGHILIGHTS

1. On April 30, 1946 Bob Feller pitched his second career no-hitter on the road against the Yankees. It was Bob Lemon who saved the day. Late in the game Lemon made a diving grab in centerfield and he recorded a double play.

2. Cleveland had one of the top pitching rotations in MLB. Lemon started his Minor League career as an infielder but found his way to the pitcher's mound in 1946.

3. 1948 was his best season. He won 20 games, struck out 147 and pitched 293 2/3 total innings. Lemon also recorded his first and only no-hitter in Detroit.

4. Had Bob Lemon not made the switch from position player to pitcher, the Indians may not have two World Series titles. 1948 was his first full season as a starting pitcher and Lemon earned two wins in the World Series including the decisive game 6 in Boston.

5. Lemon's pitching numbers in 1948; 20 wins, 20 complete games, 10 complete game shutouts, ranked him 5th in the American League MVP voting.

6. On Opening Day April 14, 1953 Lemon nearly tied Bob Feller's Opening Day no-hitter feat. Playing the same team,

the Chicago White Sox, Minnie Minoso singled to start the very first inning and Chicago went hitless after that.

7. On June 30, 1948 Lemon pitched a no-hitter and the Indians won 2-0 at Briggs Stadium in Detroit.

8. Bob Lemon, a two- time World Series Champion, earned a second ring as the New York Yankees manager beating the Los Angeles Dodgers in 6 games. His team won the final game 7-2 again on the road.

CHAPTER 6

JACKIE 42 ROBINSON

(Born January 31, 1919 Died October 24, 1972)

MAJOR LEAGUE BASEBALL has been played for more than a century. The National League, baseball's first official professional league, began in 1869. The American League's first regular season game was played in 1901. From baseball's early days it has been played in cities and towns, in rural and urban America, near corn fields and Civil War battlefields. It quickly became one of the most popular sports played in America. The game has also produced some of the greatest names in sports history: Babe Ruth, Ty Cobb, Bob Feller and many more. Between 1901-1945 countless ballplayers have made a name for themselves, some have won League MVP awards; others have played and won the World Series; still others have been inducted into Cooperstown, Baseball's Hall of Fame. Not every ballplayer played for the best team or had the most successful careers. But to that point, one thing for sure was since the first season was played, every player in the Major-Leagues was white. For the players, baseball was more than a game, it was a way of life. Teams played together, ate together, and traveled together. It was not until the spring of 1945 that the Brooklyn Dodgers General Manager had a plan to change the game forever.

African Americans were kept out of baseball since its inception, their only chance of playing professional ball was for the Negro Leagues. In 1945 the Brooklyn Dodger's general manager Branch Rickey was searching for both a way to put more fans in the seats, and for an opportunity to break the legacy of racism in baseball. Branch was looking for an African American, or at the time called "negro', to play for his team. The one question was who? Branch had made a convincing argument to his staff by saying, "baseball people, and that includes myself, are slow to change and accept new ideas. I remember that it took years to persuade them to put numbers on uniforms."[9]

A shortstop by the name of Jackie Robinson played for the Kansas City Monarchs and Branch was scouting him from afar. Branch liked what he saw in Jackie not just from his play but also his character. Robinson was a player with a quick first step on the basepaths. He also argued with umpires when calls did not go in his favor, a quick temper was Jackie's reputation. Branch called that 'spirit' and knew he had found the right player. On August 28, 1945 Rickey invited Jackie to his office to offer him a chance to play Major League Baseball. Robinson was unsure why he had come all the way to Brooklyn when he had a game to play in Chicago. Mr. Rickey told Robinson of his plans to have him play for the Brooklyn Dodgers. First, he would play with the Minor League Montreal Royals in the spring of 1946. Branch was clear with Robinson saying people are not going to be for Blacks playing on the all-white Major League teams; that fans and players alike would do anything to get him to react to their derisive rants. Rickey knew if Jackie returned a verbal curse with a curse, or followed a cheap shot with a blow of his own everyone would say Jackie could not handle the pressure or the white man's game. Rickey warned Jackie that he had to take whatever insult or injury was thrown at him, that he could not meet his opponent on his own low ground. Branch Rickey wanted a player like Jackie who could not only play the game at a high level, but also respond to all the critics and racists at a high level. Robinson assured Mr. Rickey that he could overcome any vitriol that would be thrown at him. Players, reporters, and baseball fans would relentlessly attempt to get Robinson to react, but Robinson believed that he could handle all that was thrown at him, so he accepted the offer.

On October 23, 1945, the official announcement was made that Rickey signed Jackie Robinson and would be assigned to the Montreal Royals for the 1946 season. Robinson reported for his first spring training in 1946 and joining him was Wendell Smith, a young sports journalist for a newspaper called the Pittsburgh Courier, a popular newspaper within the Black community. Wendell followed Robinson around every day on and off the field because Jackie was not the only person with something to prove. Mr. Smith would attend his ballgames and sit in the stands with his typewriter on his lap because they did not allow African Americans in the press box.

During his first and only Minor-League season Jackie exceeded expectations. With 444 at-bats Robinson collected 155 hits, drove home 66 RBI's, and batted an impressive .349 average. With his speed he stole 40 bases and was thrown out only15 times. In Mr. Rickey's eyes Robinson had earned a spot on the 1947 Dodgers roster, but that does not mean he was accepted. The Dodger's players created a petition to try and keep Robinson in Montreal, but manager Leo Durocher made it clear to the players that they would accept Jackie, or they would be traded. On April 11, 1947 Jackie Robinson signed his first Major League contract with the Brooklyn Dodgers worth $5,000.00.

On opening day April 15, 1947 Brooklyn played host to the Boston Braves at Ebbets Field. Before the season started Robinson had switched from shortstop to first base and when he took the field the fans including the hometown faithful were expressing their hatred towards Robinson. Boston's shortstop Dick Culler led off the game and Robinson was on the backend of a 5-3 groundout. The Braves were kept scoreless on a strikeout and a fly out and the home team Dodgers would bat next. Robinson stepped up to the plate searching for his first big-league hit, but he grounded out to third base and had to turn back to the dugout. Robinson was declared out at first base, but he had beaten the throw by a mile. Although the umpire was not playing by the rules Jackie could not argue or make a scene, the contract he had signed forbade it and Jackie was going to prove the naysayers wrong. Trailing 3-2 in the bottom of the 7th he was one of three runs to come home after he made it to first base on a throwing error. The final tally was 5-3 as Robinson and the Dodgers rallied to take game one of the series and the season. Robinson went hitless in his Major League debut, he batted 3 times did not walk or strike out. It was not picture perfect, but the Dodgers were in the win column.

A week following Jackie's debut on April 22 the Philadelphia Phillies traveled to Brooklyn to square off against Robinson for the first time. While Robinson was focused on winning, the Phillies manager Ben Chapman tried to make Robinson's day at the plate as miserable as possible. Chapman instructed his pitchers to hit Jackie with a pitch if they fell behind in the count 3-0, he shouted racial slurs from the Philadelphia dugout every single time Robinson came to the plate, shouting, "…you're not here to play ball. You're here to make Mr. Ricky rich. This is a white man's game; you don't belong here…"[9]. Robinson nearly succumbed and started a fight with Chapman, but he turned away and held his anger. The game was scoreless as Robinson led off the bottom of the 8th inning, and Robinson hit a soft single that fell for a hit between second base and right field. Robinson then stole second and third on a wild throw by the catcher and the Dodgers had their best scoring chance of the game. The Dodger's left fielder

Gene Hermanski slapped a base-hit to left field and Robinson scored the first run which also decided the game. The Philadelphia Phillies organization received a lot of criticism for their actions that day, and it followed them for the remainder of the season. The players and coaches from the city of Brotherly Love were not the only ones expressing their hatred. It did not matter that Robinson was helping Brooklyn win. The color of his skin caused some of his teammates to demand trades. Mr. Ricky did his best to make arrangements for the players who wanted out if they gave it their all while they were still playing for his team.

On and off the field Mr. Ricky was Jackie's voice, his outspoken leader. The Dodgers were scheduled to play Philadelphia again in May, this time on the road. Branch was phoned by the Phillies general manager Herb Pennock who refused to take the field if Robinson was in the starting lineup. When the series began Robinson collected 4 hits and 2 RBI's in a 4-2 victory. The Dodgers and the Phillies split the series 2-2 and Robinson collected 7 more hits for a total of 11 in the series, but the national backlash against Chapman was so great that he was ordered to pose for a picture with Robinson at the end of the series. For the entire season, Brooklyn's opponents showed their hatred towards Robinson, and Jackie led Major League Baseball in hit by pitches. Players would intentionally step on his ankle as they raced to first base even though they were thrown out. In many of the games played on the road the game essentially became a sideshow to the frenzy. Jackie's teammates were also not welcome in restaurants or hotels and before an important series in Cincinnati Jackie's teammate Pee Wee Reese presented a hate letter to Mr. Ricky that he had received from his family. Branch was not impressed and showed Pee Wee more letters that the Dodger organization had received; piles of letters expressing how much fans hated Robinson including death threats towards Robinson, Rickey, and his family. Fans at the Reds game were relentless in their insults hurled toward Robinson and his teammates as the Dodgers took the field for their warmups. The Cincinnati fans barked racial slurs at Robinson. The abuse came from nearly every section in the stadium when Pee Wee Reese walked over to Robinson to show the world that he put winning before race. Placing his arm around Robinson he said to Jackie, "Maybe one day we will all wear 42. That way they won't be able to tell us apart."[10] Brooklyn beat Cincinnati that game 6-5 and Robinson collected a hit in 3 at bats and scored once.

Jackie would steal second base and he would often be ruled safe, but the opposing player who applied the tag would often punch Jackie until he was ejected. Robinson ignored the abuse and kept playing ball. His positive spirit warmed the hearts of his teammates and many fans. Young boys in Brooklyn would imitate his batting routine. For many African Americans Jackie Robinson was their hero. The Brooklyn Dodgers went on a hot streak in the final month of the season and finished at 94-60, in first place five games better than their rivals the St. Louis Cardinals. Jackie Robinson played all but three games during his rookie season for the Dodgers. From day one, his great play helped him to overcome abuse from all directions. Robinson's ability to focus on winning instead of fighting made him a team leader.

Robinson finished his rookie season with 12 home runs and 48 RBI's. His speed helped him to a National League leading 29 stolen bases. Robinson's average at the plate was a high .297 and an on base percentage of .383. The Brooklyn Dodgers won the National League pennant but fell to the New York Yankees in the World Series. At the end of the year Jackie was awarded baseball's very first rookie of the year award. Whether fans had welcomed Jackie or not, the man who broke baseball's color barrier had already achieved greatness.

Robinson played his 10-year career with the Brooklyn Dodgers. Between 1949-1954 he made the All-Star roster for the National League every year. Robinson played in five more World Series and won one of them in 1955 against the Yankees.

Fifty years later, April 15, 1997 the anniversary of Robinson's debut, the Los Angeles Dodgers and the New York Mets held a ceremony prior to the first pitch to commemorate his great career. It was then that Major League Baseball retired Jack Roosevelt Robinson's number 42 across the entire league. Jackie is the only player to have his number retired by all 30 teams. Major League Baseball inducted Robinson into the Hall of Fame in 1962.

JACKIE ROBINSON'S CAREER NUMBERS.

4,877 At-Bats. 1,518 Hits. 947 Runs Scored. 137 Home Runs.
734 RBI's. .311 Batting Average

CAREER HIGHLIGHTS

1. On April 15, 1947 Jackie Robinson became the first African American to play Major League Baseball as he made his debut with the Brooklyn Dodgers.

2. During his rookie season Jackie overcame hatred and helped carry the Dodgers to a pennant winning season. Robinson became the first African American to play in a World Series.

3. Robinson's talent did not keep fans and some teammates from hating on him. The Dodgers organization received a lot of threats and Robinson led baseball in hit by pitches.

4. Jackie won baseball's very first Rookie of the year award. He collected 12 home runs and 48 RBI's. Jackie swiped 29 bases and had a slugging percentage of .427.

5. In just his third season in 1949 he became the National League's batting champion. Robinson finished with 203 hits, 16 home runs, and 124 runs driven in.

6. Branch Ricky, the man who told Robinson he had to turn the other cheek if he wanted to last, said to him after three seasons. "Now you can be yourself."[11]

7. Robinson and the Dodgers won the 1955 World Series against the New York Yankees. Brooklyn won the seventh game 2-0 at Yankee Stadium.

8. On April 15, 2004 Major League Baseball began a new tradition known as "Jackie Robinson Day." A day that commemorates Jackie's historic accomplishments and of becoming the first African American to play Major League Baseball. Each year on Jackie Robinson Day every player on all the Major League teams dons the retired number 42 in honor of Jackie Robinson's career that changed the league forever.

Pitcher Mel Harder: Four Time All-Star 13
All Star innings, 0 runs allowed

Earl Averill: 1938 All-Star Game, Crosley Field Cincinnati, OH

"Rapid Robert" Bob Feller: The one and only
opening day no-hitter, April 16, 1940

Indians short stop and player manager Lou Boudreau 1942-1950

Bob Lemon: 1948 World Series Champion 2-0 Series record

Jackie Robinson and Phillies manager Ben Chapman

Larry Doby: First African American to play
MLB in the American League

Frank Robinson: First African American
Manager in MLB History, 1975

Jim Thome: power hitter. Franchise record 52 home runs in 2002

The Fans: 455 Consecutive Sellout Streak 1995-2001

CHAPTER 7

LARRY 14 DOBY

(Born December 13, 1923 Died June 18, 2003)

IT IS NOT often that you are remembered for coming in second. For Larry Doby that is what happened when he arrived in the Major Leagues after Jackie Robinson. Larry Doby was born in Camden, South Carolina to father Dave Doby and mother Etta Brooks. Larry's father was a traveling horse groomer and a semi-pro baseball player, which ultimately led to his parents divorcing, and when he was 8 years old, Larry's father died in a drowning accident in New York. During those difficult times, his mother moved to Paterson, New Jersey looking for work. Larry was left behind to live with his grand-mother, and later with his aunt and uncle. Growing up in the Palmetto State he received an education at Boylan Haven-Mather Academy which was affiliated with the Methodist Church. During his time at the Academy Doby learned to play a variety of sports including bas-ketball and baseball. By the age of 14, Doby was ready to attend high school so he returned home to live near his mother in New Jersey. Between 1938-1942 the young teen studied at Paterson Eastside High School to become a physical education teacher. He also continued to play sports and earned 11 varsity letters in football, basketball, baseball, and track where was the only Black player for every single sport. His football team won the state championship and was invited to play in Florida, but the promoters refused to let Doby play in the game. As a gesture of solidarity his High School teammates decided to forego the trip instead.

Before graduating high school Doby played baseball for the Black semi-pro baseball team the Smart Sets, and a professional basketball team called the Harlem Renaissance. With his athleticism he was awarded a basketball scholarship and chose to enroll at Long Island University in Brooklyn. Doby later admitted that the main reason he chose LIU was to stay close to his High School sweetheart, Helyn Curvy whom he had dated in high school. Before enrolling at Long Island University Doby also played in the Negro Leagues for the Newark Eagles. He played the position of second base under the name Larry Walker to protect his college amateur status and instantly became a star when he batted around .391 in his first season.

Doby was drafted by the United States Navy in 1943. (20). While in the Navy, Doby was assigned to serve at Camp Robert Smalls: the black division for the Great Lakes Naval Training Station in Illinois. He stayed in shape and continued to train to become a physical education instructor. He also played hoops and baseball during his free time but continued to have dreams of playing Major League Baseball. By the year 1946 Larry was released from his services and returned to New Jersey. That same year he rejoined the Eagles baseball team and helped defeat the Kansas City Monarchs in the Negro League World Series where Doby batted .372 with a home run, five RBI and three stolen bases in seven games. He finished the season ranked 4th in batting average and 2nd in home runs with 9. During the off-season he married Helyn on August 10th, 1946 in Paterson. Many players, coaches and fans of the Negro Leagues thought that

Larry Doby might be the first man to crack the color barrier of the Major Leagues.

Doby heard the news about the Dodgers signing Jackie Robinson and that Robinson would likely play in the Majors in the spring of 1947. The news of Robinson becoming the first African American in the Majors motivated Larry to stick with baseball. "My main thing was to become a teacher and a coach. But when I heard about Jackie, I decided to concentrate on baseball. I forgot about going back to college."[12] The Cleveland Indians owner Bill Veeck took notice of Larry's talent and made plans to sign the second basemen after the All-Star break. Cleveland quickly and quietly bought his contract and Doby was scheduled to make his debut on July 10, 1947. When news broke out about Veeck's decision to sign a Black man, Doby's debut was moved up to July 5. The Indians were playing in Chicago when Doby joined the team and when player-manager Lou Boudreau walked him into the clubhouse, his new teammates chose to ignore him. He was not welcomed immediately. "I knew it was segregated times, but I had never seen anything like that in athletes. I was embarrassed. it was tough."[13] Lou Boudreau. Two days later the Indians began their three-game series facing the White Sox at Comiskey Park. After six innings of baseball the Indians had a 5-1 hill to climb. Player-manager Lou Boudreau called for Doby to pinch-hit hoping the rookie could provide a spark. This moment marked the first time an African American played Major League Baseball in the American League. You only get one Major League debut and after one at-bat the pitcher Earl Harrist had himself a strikeout. The Tribe rallied but fell short losing the ballgame 6-5. Doby finished his debut batting 0-1. He had not played a full game and his new teammates were hating on him even more. Profanity was often used against Larry and occasionally the locker rooms became violent if Cleveland did not win. The following day on July 6 the Indians finished the series in doubleheader fashion. Doby sat on the bench for game one as he watched the Indians fall short to the White Sox 3-2. In game two he made his first start as a first basemen hoping he could make a strong impression. Batting in the top of the 3rd with the lead, Larry grabbed a bat with runners on base. The pitch was offered and Larry singled home a run for his first big league hit and RBI. The Tribe had increased their lead to 3-1 and scored twice more to win game two 5-1. Doby batted four times in his first career start and finished with one hit and a run batted in. July 6, 1947 was Doby's only start during his rookie season. He played in 29 games and only batted .156 with 2 RBI's. During the disappointing rookie season Larry Doby pointed out. "It was 11 weeks between the time Jackie Robinson, and I came into the Majors. I can't see how things we're any different for me than they we're for him."[14]

Larry Doby's sophomore season in 1948 was also his first spring training with the Cleveland Indians. The outfield coach Bill McKechnie encouraged Doby to take on the role of playing centerfield so he studied books on that position so he would be ready by opening day. During his first full season some of his teammates still were not in favor of playing with a Black man. Larry continued to be verbally abused by the crowd and other teams. He went through the same tumult as Robinson despite having a highly productive season. The Tribe got off to a hot start at the beginning of the season winning their first 6 games while playing 5 games on the road. On April 23, 1948 game two of the young season was played at Briggs Stadium with the Indians facing the Detroit Tigers. In the top of the 3rd inning, Larry Doby smashed his first career home run. It was the first run of the game and Cleveland pounded their rivals by a score of 8-2. Doby collected three hits in five at-bats and scored twice. During those first six games the Indians outscored their opponents 40-20. In his first six games Doby reached base with 9 hits, 2 home runs and 5 runs batted in. It was early but in 30 at-bats, every pitcher he faced had failed to strike him out. The young outfielder's early success lasted for the entire season and his numbers showed it. Doby played in 121 games and finished with a .301 batting average. In his first full season Larry homered 14 times and drove in 66-runs. He scored 83 times and tripled 9 times. His prodigious swing could find the gap all over the diamond.

The Cleveland Indians finished the 1948 season with a record of 97-58 and would square off against the Red Sox to decide the 1948 champion of the American League. The Indians traveled to Fenway Park to play a tiebreaker against the Boston Red Sox. A win for Boston would set up an all Boston World Series against the Braves. On the night of October 4, 1948, it was win or go home. Early in the game, the Indians were deadlocked with both sides only scoring a single run. Batting in the top of the 4th, Cleveland's bats exploded with 4-runs to take the lead for good. Larry Doby smacked a double into center field and scored on an infield groundout by Jim Hegan for the team's fourth run of the game. The Red Sox failed to make up ground and watched the Indians steal the pivotal championship game in front of their home fans. With an 8-3 victory, the Cleveland Indians had punched their ticket to the World Series for the first time since 1920.

A sellout crowd at Braves Field witnessed their Braves win game 1 on October 6 in a pitching duel. The Indians pitcher Bob Feller gave up the game's lone run as he got no run support. The Tribe lost the first game but did not roll over. Game 2 was played the follow-ing night and they re-tied the series with a 4-1 road win. In the top of the 4th centerfielder Larry Doby collected an RBI single that gave Cleveland the lead for good. On October 9 the fourth game of the se-ries was the second game played in Cleveland. The Braves had fallen behind 2-games to 1 looking to return the favor and take a road game. Thousands of loyal fans watched their Tribe battle and take a 3-games to 1 lead with a slim 2-1 victory. Early in the bottom of the 3rd inning Doby smoked a home run to the right field seats that tallied the teams second run. With that powerful swing, Doby had become the first African American to hit a home run in the World Series. The Braves did not go away as they beat up the Indians in game-5 with an 11-5 win in Cleveland. The Indians traveled back to Boston in hopes of avoiding a game 7. Larry Doby had a solid game six with 2 hits, but no runs scored and a strikeout. His teammates were able to pick him up and win game-6 to clinch the World Series, making Larry Doby the first Black man to win a baseball World Series Championship. Doby played in every game and finished with a home run and 2 runs batted in. The Cleveland Indians franchise has played in 6 World Series, the most recent matchup came in 2016 facing the Chicago Cubs. Cleveland has not won the World Series since that 1948 season.

The next season in 1949 was the start of seven consecutive All Star appearance for the center fielder. Most of Doby's mid-summer classic matchups were quiet as the National League won 5 of the 7 All Star Games that he played in. One of his teams two wins came in 1954 played at Cleveland Municipal stadium in Cleveland. Doby's historic career lasted from 1947-1959. He played 10 seasons with the Indians. The Cleveland Indians retired Lawrence Eugene Doby's number (14) in 1994. Major League Baseball inducted Doby into the Hall of Fame in 1998.

LARRY DOBY'S CAREER NUMBERS.

5,348 At-Bats. 1,515 Hits. 960 Runs Scored. 253 Home Runs.
970 RBI's. .283 Batting Average

CAREER HIGHLIGHTS

1. On July 5, 1947, Larry Doby made his Major League debut pinch-hitting as the first African American to play for the Cleveland Indians and the American League, and the first player to go directly from the Negro Leagues to the Major Leagues.

2. In his first full season with Cleveland, Doby batted .301 with 14 home runs and 66 RBI's. The centerfielder helped beat the Red Sox on the road to earn a trip to the World Series.

3. The Indians won the World Series in 6 games against the Boston Braves. Game-4 in Cleveland, Doby became the first African American to blast a home run in the World Series. The Indians won the game 2-1.

4. The decisive game six of the 1948 World Series was played in Boston and the Indians won by the slimmest of margins 4-3. Larry Doby became the first African American to win a World Series.

5. His third season in 1949 was the first of seven straight All Star Game appearances. (1949-1955.)

6. After the 1954 season Larry Doby ranked 2nd in American League MVP voting. Larry tied a career high with 32 home

runs and his best 126 RBI's. Yogi Berra of the Yankees was the AL MVP with 10 less home runs and one less RBI. (22 HR 125 RBI) His .307 batting average beat him.

7. Larry Doby and the Indians made it back to the World Series in 1954. Over the course of 154 regular season games the Indians finished with a record of 111-43 by far the team's best season. Cleveland got swept in 4-games by the New York Giants.

8. During his career Doby had come in second twice. When he joined the Indians after the Dodgers signed Jackie, and he had become the second black manager in baseball behind Frank Robinson. Larry Doby became the White Sox manager in 1978.

CHAPTER 8

FRANK 20 ROBINSON

(Born August 31, 1935 Died February 7, 2019)

THE CLEVELAND INDIANS greatest career players did not always start their careers with the Cleveland Indians. Frank Robinson was an African American baseball player who began his 21-year career with the Cincinnati Redlegs. Robinson made his debut on opening day April 17, 1956. During his rookie season, he put up numbers great enough to play for the National League All-Stars. The Redlegs ended the season with a record of 91-63. Highly respectable but the team fell to third place in their division and missed the playoffs. Robinson played in 152 games, he homered 38 times, and batted an impressive .290 average on the season. At that time, his 38-home runs tied a record most home runs hit by a rookie. His RBI total was 83 and by the end of the season, he was named rookie of the year.

When Robinson's sixth season rolled around in 1961, the Redlegs had become the modern-day Cincinnati Reds. In the month of July, Frank Robinson batted .409 with 13 home runs. He plated 34-runs and was named the National League's player of the month. The Reds won the League pennant but lost to the Yankees 4-games to 1 in the World Series. He ended the season with 37 home runs, 124 runs driven in, and a .323 average and the young star was named MVP of the National League. After the 1965 season, the Reds had some of the best batters in baseball but were desperate to get good pitching and traded Robinson to Baltimore. The Orioles acquired the outfielder Frank Robinson, and he continued his success as a member of the American League and his first season with the Orioles was by far his best in the Major Leagues. With 576 at-bats, Robinson led the American League with 49 homers, 122- RBI's, and he had a batting average of .316. Those impressive league leading categories earned Frank Robinson baseball's Triple-Crown award. Robinson became a seven time All-Star over a 10-year span and was also awarded the American League MVP award in 1966 becoming the first and only player to date to be named Most Valuable Player in both leagues. Award winning seasons had become a regular thing over his early career. If becoming a two-time MVP was not enough for the star as Robinson and the Baltimore Orioles swept the Los Angeles Dodgers in the 1966 World Series. Three of the four victories were shutouts, two wins were 1-0 in front of a home crowed. Robinson had become the first position player to be named Most Valuable Player of a World Series. His play helped the Orioles capture the team's first title in franchise history. It was also the final year before the Commissioner's trophy came into existence. Robinson collected 4 hits, 3 RBI's and 2 home runs and his second homer came in game 4, it was the only run of the game. The Orioles outscored the Dodgers 13-2, the fewest runs scored by the losing side in World Series history.

Four years following the Orioles title, Robinson and the Birds played and beat the Reds in the 1970 World Series. Baltimore clinched a second Fall Classic Crown over a five-game stretch winning the last game 9-3 on October 15. Frank Robinson's final season with Baltimore came in 1971 and by 1974 when he was with the Angels, Robinson was traded to the Cleveland Indians. The trade to

Cleveland came late in the season when the Indians were already out of playoff contention. Robinson was persuaded to continue playing although he was past his prime. As the 1975 season was just around the corner Frank Robin was named baseball's first Black manager by the Cleveland Indians. April 8, 1975 was opening day played at home against the New York Yankees. Robinson didn't play often in his two full years with the Indians, but it was this moment that stands out if you are a Tribe fan. With no score in the bottom of the 1st, player-manager Frank Robinson drove a ball over the left field wall in his first at-bat as a player-manager for a 1-0 lead. The Indians won the season opener 5-3 and player-manager Robinson made history. The Cleveland Indians retired Frank Robinson Jr.'s number (20) in 2017. Major League Baseball inducted Robinson into the Hall of Fame in 1982.

FRANK ROBINSON'S CAREER NUMBERS.

10,006 At-Bats. 2,943 Hits. 1,829 Runs Scored. 586 Home Runs.
1,812 RBI's. .294 Batting Average

CAREER HIGHLIGHTS

1. Playing as a rookie with the 1956 Redlegs, Frank Robinson tied the record for most home runs hit by a rookie with 38.

2. After his rookie season Robinson was named NL rookie of the year with 38 home runs, 83 RBI's and a .290 batting average.

3. Shortly after his first season Frank Robinson was named the National League MVP in 1961 as a member of the Reds.

4. At the start of the 1966 season Robinson played for the Orioles in the American League. Robinson won his second MVP trophy collecting two MVP awards, one from each league.

5. In 1966 in his first season with the Orioles, Robinson won the regular season MVP, a World Series title and was named the World Series Most Valuable Player with two clutch home runs.

6. Playing from 1956-1976 Frank Robinson was a 14 time All-Star.

7. Before the start of the 1975 season, Cleveland chose Frank Robinson as the team's player-manager. With this new title to his name, Robinson had become baseball's first black manager.

8. Opening day on April 8, 1975 player manager Frank Robinson hit a solo home run in his first at-bat as a manager. The Tribe won the ballgame against the Yankees 5-3.

CHAPTER 9

JIM 25 THOME

(Born August 27, 1970)

JIM THOME WAS born in Peoria, Illinois, a minute or two after his twin sister Jenny, making him the youngest of five children. Several members of the Thome family were talented softball players; Jim's grandpa Chuck, his Uncle Art, and Aunt Carolyn are all member of the Fast Pitch Wing sports Hall of Fame loaded in Peoria. Roughly 40-years before Jimmy was born, his grandpa considered playing Major League Baseball, but he had no real opportunity due to his work. Growing up, Jim's two older brothers Chuck III and Randy passed down their knowledge of the game to Jim and it was recommended by his brother Randy to take swings from the left side of the plate. Randy told his brother that left-handed batters produce more power, and the rest Is history. His brothers also explained to Jim the importance of staying focused during high pressure moments. Focus would play a key factor in Jim's future success and at a young age, he did not take these lessons for granted.

Thome loved to wake early most mornings to work on improving his swing. He would step outside with his bat on the driveway and swing away with rocks that he piled up. It became an unpleasant routine for the neighbors and one morning his swing broke a window of a nearby house. Jimmy's father Chuck paid for the broken window and decided he would contribute to his son's love for the game. Chuck Thome worked many long days for Caterpillar Inc., a company that manufactured construction vehicles like bulldozers. Although he worked hard and often, his father found the time to pitch to Jim and help him work on his fielding.

In the fall of 1984, Thome began his freshmen year at Limestone High School located in Bartonville, Peoria County where Thome played basketball and baseball. On the court one season, his team the Rockets won a conference championship and Thome put up 36 points in the triple overtime victory. When he was a junior, he played the position of shortstop and he blasted 12 home runs which led all high schoolers in the state of Illinois. Major League teams started to take interest; the Cincinnati Reds scouted him the most, but they made no offer.

Shortly after graduation Thome enrolled at Illinois Central College (ICC) where he continued to play baseball and basketball. After one season playing for ICC Thome was drafted in the 13th round by the Cleveland Indians and was assigned to the Gulf Coast League Indians for the 1989 season. In his first year in the minors, Thome was unimpressive, posting a .237 batting average, no home runs and only 22 runs batted in. But it was then that Thome met Charlie Manuel, the legendary hitting guru who changed Thome's career. Manual saw a natural hitter, and someone who could develop into a power hitter the Tribe was looking for. After much coaching and hard work, for the 1990 season Thome raised his average to .340 and stroked 16 home runs and 50 RBI's. Thome attributed some of his success in part to Manuel's convincing Thome to point his bat to center field before each pitch to relax himself; that pose became Thome's trademark look.

For most of the 1960's, '70's and '80's the Cleveland Indians were an average ballclub at best, and often perennial 'cellar dwellers'. But with the 331st pick in the 1989 MLB draft, the Cleveland Indians selected Jim Thome in the 13th round, and the fortunes of the club began to change. Thome was quickly moving through the rankings as he was promoted to play Class A-baseball. The rising infield star continued to swing a .300 average and by the seasons end he was given the Lou Boudreau award. This recognition is made annually to Cleveland's best minor league player. Starting in 1991 Thome advanced to Class-AA and became the full time third basemen for the Akron Aeros. The slugger's home run total decreased slightly but he maintained a .300 batting average. Jim eventually made it to Class-AAA and soon after, was called up by the Indians in early September 1991. The Cleveland Indians were playing on the road on September 4, 1991 when Jim Thome made his Major League debut. The Indians defeated the Twins 8-4 at the Metrodome and their new third basemen Thome had an effective debut. Thome batted .500 with 4 at-bats and he scored a run and collected his first RBI. One month later, on October 4 the Tribe played at Yankee Stadium where they had less than a full series to play before their season was over. With more than 100 losses to their name the future was uncertain for their club. The rookie Jim Thome batted with two outs in the top of the 9th inning. He faced the Yankee closer Steve Farr and needed to come through with something. The hurler offered his pitch and Thome crushed a 2-run homer into the upper deck for a late 3-2 lead! His first career home run was as clutch as they come, and the Yankees did not score in their final at-bats. The Indians won the game and what a moment for the young power hitter. Thome played in 27 games during his rookie campaign and in his 98 at-bats he homered once and drove in 9 runs. With a .255 average, little did the franchise know that Thome was about to embark on one of the greatest displays of power in franchise history.

When Jim Thome entered the league, he played home games with the Indians at Municipal Stadium, but to start of the 1994 season the Cleveland Indians officially called Jacobs Field their new home. The Indians had one of their best lineups in years with rising stars such as Kenny Lofton, Carlos Baerga, Sandy Alomar Jr., Manny Ramirez, Jim Thome and more. The city and the organization believed they had a real chance to win the League Pennant even though the Indians had not made a playoff appearance since 1954. This was Thome's fourth season with the Indians and Manuel and teammate Eddie Murray helped him to evolve into a real power threat.

On July 22, 1994, the Indians battled their rivals the White Sox at Jacobs Field. The White Sox pitcher Jason Bere made his offer to Thome who hit a deep drive to center field over the fence. In the bottom of the 2nd inning Thome stepped up again before the inning was over and crushed a second home run into the bullpen. The Tribe third baseman led off the 5th inning and the pitcher looked worried as he prepared to make his pitch. The offer was made and Thome drove the ball to deep right field again and gone! Three hits, three RBI's, and three home runs! Fireworks shot into the air as he rounded the bases and scored to give the Indians a 9-6 lead. The final score was 9-8 as the Tribe won a nail biter with the help of their slugger.

During the 1994 season the Indians were one of the hottest teams in baseball and their record reflected it. In a normal regular season, every club played 162 games, however, in August the Indians and the rest of the players went on strike because the owners wanted to limit every team to a restricted salary cap. That year the Indians finished 66-47 with 49 games still to be played, although the Tribe had seemed to find their groove, because of the strike there would be no playoffs or World Series during the 1994 season.

Baseball resumed play in 1995 for another shortened season after the strike. For the Indians fans that never experienced the magical season, radio announcer Tom Hamilton summed it up often sounded like this: 'The pitch, a swing and a drive to deep right field, away back, gone for Thome!' Or 'Thome swings and blast that ball to deep left field and gone to the bleachers!' Every player contributed to the team's success, but Jim Thome crushed 25- home runs and knocked in 73 RBI's. His batting average was well above three hundred at .314. After a 41-year playoff drought, a packed Jacobs Field anxiously awaited the final out that would clinch the division. As Tom Hamilton called the play, "In the air, Thome at third, and the season of dreams has become a reality! Cleveland, you will have an October to remember! The 1995 American League Central Division Champs." [15] (Tom Hamilton). Jim Thome and the Cleveland Indians had swept the Red Sox and beaten the Mariners to clinch the American League pennant for the first time since 1954.

On the journey to the World Series Jim Thome played in 8 games, smoked 3-home runs and collected 8 RBI's. Unfortunately for Jimmy and the city of Cleveland, the Indians lost to the Atlanta Braves in a six game World Series battle. Thome and the Tribe made it back to the World Series in 1997 but fell short again with an even greater heartbreak. In game 7, the Indians pitcher Jose Mesa allowed the tying run to come home in the Marlins final at-bat. The Indians lost the game in 11 innings 3-2.

Jim Thome played 22 seasons in the Major Leagues, 13 years with the Cleveland Indians. His career with the Tribe was one of the greatest displays of home run power the franchise had ever seen. The Cleveland Indians retired James Howard Thome's number (25) in 2018. Major League Baseball inducted Thome into the Hall of Fame in 2018. This author was one of 35,000 fans that witnessed the pre-game ceremony and all who attended heard what he had to say. "To have my jersey retired gives me the chills. To see my number hanging in the rafters of the company of Bob Feller, Lou Boudreau, Jackie Robinson, Mel Harder, Larry Doby, Earl Averill, Bob Lemon, and Frank Robinson. I don't really know what to say. That's some field of dream stuff right there."[16] (Jim Thome)

JIM THOME'S CAREER NUMBERS

8,422 At-Bats. 2,328 Hits. 1,583 Runs Scored. 612 Home Runs.
1,699 RBI's. .276 Batting Average

CAREER HIGHLIGHTS

1. Jim Thome's power made him a Hall of Fam Player, Thome hit 612 home runs in his career, 337 as a member of the Cleveland Indians.

2. Jim Thome holds the Major League record most walk-off homers with 13. He hit 9 of them with the Cleveland Indians.

3. During the 2002 season Jim Thome hit 52 home runs which broke the franchise record formally held by Albert Belle who hit 50 in 1995.

4. On June 15, 1994, the Indians faced the Blue Jays at home and won in extra innings 4-3. Jim Thome hit the first walk-off home run in Jacobs Field history, a solo home run in the bottom of the 13th inning. With that win the Tribe had swept Toronto

5. On October 15, 1995 in game five of the ALCS, Jim Thome hit the go-ahead 2-run home run against the Mariners in the bottom of the 6th. Cleveland won the game 3-2 thanks to his dinger.

6. Nine Major League batters have hit 600 or more home runs. On August 15, 2011 Jim Thome hit home runs 599 and 600 as a member of the Minnesota Twins.

7. On July 3, 1999, the Indians power hitter Jim Thome smashed a home run that literally left the ballpark. Facing the Royals, the ball carried over the wall in centerfield and onto the sidewalk. The distance was measured at 511 feet, the longest home run hit at Jacobs Field.

8. On August 2, 2014 Jim Thome and the Cleveland Indians unveiled a 12-foot bronze statue in his likeness. He also signed a one-day contract to officially retire as a member of the Cleveland Indians.

CHAPTER **10**

THE 455 FANS

ON APRIL 4, 1994, there was hype and hope all around Cleveland, Ohio on a Monday afternoon like none in recent memory. It was Major League Baseball's opening day 41,459 diehard Indians fans made their way to their seats at Jacobs Field; Cleveland's brand-new ballpark. On that day the Indians squared off against the Seattle Mariners, a highly talented team. Dennis Martinez started on the hill for the Indians and in the top of the 1st he surrendered the first run for an early 1-0 Seattle lead. By the bottom of the 8th inning, the sellout crowd had grown restless, not only were the Indians getting shutout 2-0, but the Mariners pitcher Randy Johnson was pitching a gem. Johnson was 6 outs away from pitching an opening day no-hitter that would tie the record set by Indians legend Bob Feller. Johnson issued a walk and Indian's catcher Sandy Alomar Jr. batted with a runner on first as he slapped a hit through the right side to break up the no-hitter. The runners moved up on a wild pitch and then the right Fielder Manny Ramirez doubled home both runs as he lined a ball high off the left field wall. The stadium had come to life as the fans were standing and cheering loudly. The game was tied 2-2 and the go-ahead run was in scoring position. In the bottom of the 11th the Indians prepared to bat with the score now showing 3-3. Kevin King was pitching for the Mariners and a 1 out double by Indians first

83

baseman Eddie Murray gave the Tribe a golden opportunity to win. A fly out by the designated hitter Paul Sorrento followed by an intentional walk set up Wayne Kirby for an at-bat with the winning run just 90 -feet away. Kirby swung at the pitch and won the game with a walk- off single that he lined into left field for a 4-3 season opener victory! The debut of Jacobs Field was complete! The Indians won in dramatic walk-off fashion and there were hugs and high fives all around home plate. The fans were cheering and celebrating, nobody wanted to leave. The fan base of Cleveland was coming alive, with a new ballpark, exciting players, and the hopes of a long-suffering town for a championship. But after only 113 games, with the Indians only 1 game out of first place in the American League Central Division, the season came to an abrupt halt with a player's strike. The fans pent up excitement, expectations and the emerging powerhouse team would have to wait another year.

The 1995 season brought high expectations for the team. For most of the previous 30 years fan attendance at Indians games ranked at or near the bottom of the 14 American League teams, with only an opening day sellout each season and annual attendance less than 1 million fans. But in 1995, with an exciting team and a gleaming new stadium, that all changed. With the team atop the Central Division, on a warm late spring night on June 12, 1995 the Cleveland Indians won a ballgame 4-3 against the Orioles in front of a sellout crowd. With the new ballpark, there were countless fans wanting to experience a game played at the Jake. Little did anybody know that every home game going from that date into 2001 would be a sellout. The streak ended on April 4, 2001, game 2 of the season on a chilly afternoon. The Indians pounded their rivals the White Sox 8-4 in front of 363.363 fans, just shy of a sellout crowd. Their 455th straight sellout streak had come to an end after 455 consecutive sellouts, a Major League Baseball record at the time. During the sellout streak the Indians sold 19,324,248 tickets. The number 455 was retired and named "The Fans" to recognize their support.

The name Jacobs Field was kept through the 2007 season, but starting in 2008, the park changed its name to Progressive Field which is its current name. In the mid 90's and early 2000's fans experienced what was known as Jacobs Field Magic. No matter the name, here are some top plays experienced by the fans at the corner of Carnegie and Ontario.

On November 2, 2016, the Indians played host to the Chicago Cubs in game 7 of the World Series. A packed Progressive Field watched as their Indians trailed 6-4 in the bottom of the 8th with a man on base. Aroldis Chapman Chicago's closer came in one inning early hoping to slam the door and keep the Tribe from tying the ballgame. Chapman was firing his 105 MPH heater and the batter Rajai Davis seemingly had little to no chance until he smoked one of the most memorable hits in Progressive Field history. "Now the pitch, swung on lined to deep left field, it is gone! You should see the celebration out of the Indians third base dugout! Rajai Davis a bullet 2-run homer down the left field line, clearing the nineteen-foot wall. We are tied at 6!" [17] Tom Hamilton

On September 14, 2017, The Indians were playing for their twenty-second consecutive win when they won the only game of the streak in walk-off fashion against the Royals. "Bruce awaiting the 2-0 pinch. Here it comes, a swing and a drive to deep right down the line base hit. Into the corner around third, coming home Ramirez it's a game winner for Jay Bruce! And history marches on! A mob scene in shallow center, Jay Bruce getting pummeled, as he smoked one down the right field line, a game winning single for Jay Bruce! And the Indians continue this improbable run! Twenty-two consecutive wins, and the Indians get their first walk-off win in the streak!" [18] Tom Hamilton

On May 23, 1999 Indians gold glove shortstop Omar Vizquel came through with his bat in the bottom of the 9th. "Vizquel today 2-4 two singles. Sexton at third, Cabrera at second, Lofton at first. Nobody sitting down at Jacobs Field. The 2-1 delivery, swung on and drilled, to deep right center, awway back gone! A home plate mobbing, Vizquel! A game winning grand slam! Omar has disappeared as the Indians have mobbed Vizquel, a game winning grand slam! Can you believe it!"[19] Tom Hamilton

On August 5, 2001, the Seattle Mariners played at Jacobs Field with the best record in baseball at 80-30. The game was practically over as the Tribe trailed 14-2 in the bottom of the 7th. With 9 outs to play with the Indians rallied and scored 12 times before the final out was made. The Indians batted in the bottom of the 11th with Kenny Lofton standing on second base as the winning run. "The pitch, swung on line drive base hit to left. Lofton around third he's going to score the game winner. McLemore's throw, the slide not in time!" [20] Tom Hamilton

On July 3, 1999 Thome hit the longest home run in Jacobs Field history against the Kansas City Royals. "Winds it up delivers. Thome drills one high and deep to center, way, way, way back. Gone deep into the picnic plaza and that might have even got out of the ballpark. Jim Thome has just left Jacobs Field onto Eagle Ave. That will take two tape measures. The Tribe down 2-1." [21] Tom Hamilton

On August 19, 2016, the Indians played host to the Toronto Blue Jays, a sneak peek at that year's pennant round in late October. Jose Ramirez smashed a game tying solo homerun into the right field seats in the bottom of the 9th. Jays pitcher Roberto Osuna was not replaced, and he faced the next batter Tyler Naquin. "A swing and a drive to deep right, Saunders at the wall. It hits off the top of the wall. Naquin's around second, he's on his way to third, he'll try to score. Here is the throw, not in time! Usain Naquin flying around the bases. On a drive off the wall in right. It ricocheted back towards the infield, and coach Mike Sarbaugh never slowed him down."[22] Tom Hamilton

On October 5, 2007, the Yankees and the Indians played game 2 of the American League Divisional Series in front of a sellout crowd at the Jake. An infestation of tiny midges descended from Lake Erie and caused a big problem for Yankees pitcher Joba Chamberlin. With the Yankees in the lead 1-0 the bugs swarmed around the mound in Chamberlin's face as he walked a batter, threw a wild pitch and after applying the bug spray gave up another wild pitch to tie the game at 1-1. Three innings later in the bottom of the 11th the Indians DH batted with the game tied, the bases loaded, and bugs flying all around. "These fans on their feet in a frenzy, Hafner climbs back in. 3-2 the count, bases loaded. Here's the pitch, swung on, line drive base hit right center, it's a game winner! Travis Hafner rips one up the ally in right center! The Indians go to New York up two games to none, and a mob scene at first base. What a ballgame!"[23] Tom Hamilton

On May 21, 2014, the Indians played in a back and forth game against their rivals the Tigers. Three times the Tigers had surrendered the game tying run in Cleveland's last at-bat to give them new life. Both clubs were tied at 10 and in the bottom of the 13th with the bases loaded and Ryan Raburn up to bat, something had to give. "And a balk, ballgame! How about that! We now have seen everything. A walk-off balk! Unbelievable! Cabrera scores the winner, on a walk-off balk! As Alburquerque started into his delivery stopped."[24] Tom Hamilton

CAREER NUMBERS
EPILOGUE

(Comeback for the Ages)

READERS SHOULD KEEP in mind that this book is about the legendary players whose retired numbers hang in the right field corner of the Home of the Cleveland Indians. However, there are two players in this final segment whom the author believes deserve to one day have their number placed beside the other immortal names at Progressive Field: Kenny Lofton and Omar Vizquel. Lofton had a strong swing and was quick on the bases and in the outfield. Vizquel played shortstop and got down and dirty making some of the most spectacular infield plays ever recorded in baseball. He was awarded the gold glove award 8 times as a member of the Cleveland Indians and 11 times overall. It takes more than two players to win a ballgame especially when you fall behind to the best team in the league, but on August 5, 2001 Lofton and Vizquel led "The Comeback".

It was stretch time at the corner of Carnegie and Ontario and most Indians fans had already left the ballpark. With the deficit at 12-runs this game was all but over. The Seattle Mariners, a team 50 games above .500 at 80-30, took an early lead and never looked back. The

Indians fell behind 4-0 after two innings and by the bottom of the 7th, the score showed 14-2 Seattle.

Aaron Sele, the M's starter, was still in the game as the Indians third basemen Russell Branyan led off the inning. He swung at the first pitch and blasted the ball as it sailed over the right field wall for a solo homer to narrow the score to 14-3. Two quick outs followed the solo blast but a base hit by catcher Einar Diaz and a walk by Kenny Lofton kept the inning going. Four straight tosses by the pitcher missed their mark and Omar Vizquel walked to load up the bases. Sele was replaced by Mariners reliever John Halama who needed to get the final out of the seventh inning. Batting with a 1-1 count the Indians second basemen Jolbert Cabrera blooped a 2-run base hit in front of the left fielder Martin to score Diaz and Kenny Lofton for a 14-5 deficit. By the end of the seventh, the Indians had scratched out 3-runs but still had a hill to climb.

The Mariners bats were silenced in the eighth, their last run scored came in the fifth on an infield groundout with one out. In the bottom of the 8th inning, the Indians first basemen Jim Thome stepped up to lead off the inning down by nine. "The 2-1, swung on hit high and deep to left back goes Martin, Martin at the wall looking up and it's gone to the home run porch! Jim Thome with his second home run tonight! Giving him a league high 36, and the Tribe down 14-6 and for Jim Thome that is multi-homer game number 4 this year."[25] Tom Hamilton. Russell Branyan, who homered his last at-bat, got to take first base as he was nicked by the hurlers offer with no outs. Fourteen to six and the Tribe was showing some signs of life but still it seemed too little too late. As he stepped to the plate Marty Cordova the right fielder batted with a runner on first: "Cordova with a drive into deep left field. This ball is going, gone to the bleachers! Marty Cordova with a 2-run homer to the bleachers in left, and it's a 14-8 game in the eighth inning."[26] Tom Hamilton A groundout was made for the first out, but Einar Diaz responded with a 1 out infield single. Kenny Lofton kept the line moving as he slapped a base hit into centerfield, Diaz advanced into scoring position.

Lou Piniella called for reliever Norm Charlton hoping his arm could silence this late game rally. Runners were on first and second base for the shortstop Omar Vizquel as Cleveland now trailed by six. "Vizquel a looping liner toward the right field line it's going to drop for a fair ball. That is going to score Diaz, Lofton into third, Vizquel into second."[27] Tom Hamilton Lofton made the attempt to swipe home as the ball got away, but he was tagged out. A strikeout ended the eighth inning and the Tribe had made up some ground, now down 14-9.

Ed Taubensee, the Indian's backup catcher, led off the inning with a single but, the Tribe was down to their last out after Norm Charlton retired Thome on a fly out and struck out Russell Branyan. Some fans were still at the game, but down by five with two men gone in the 9th, this game looked to be decided. Marty Cordova the right fielder lined a double into left field, Taubensee held up at third base as Will Cordero stepped up with two men in scoring position. Another move to the Mariners bullpen as Jeff Nelson took over trying to get the final out of the game. Cordero on a full count took a base on balls to load the bases as the heater from Nelson just barely missed the strike zone. As Tom Hamilton described it next, "Diaz at the plate with a 3-2 count, right hander against right hander, Nelson delivers. A swing and a line drive base hit to left. Taubensee scores, Cordova scores, Cordero stops at second. Diaz with his third straight hit."[28] Tom Hamilton. It was now fourteen to eleven the Indians trailed, and the tying run came to the plate. The Mariner's manager Lou Piniella switched to his closer Kazuhiro Sasaki. The Mariners who once led 14-2 in the seventh now had a save situation on their hands. Kenny

Lofton with one strike lined a single into left field. Will Cordero stopped at third base to load the basses for the winning run at the plate represented by Omar Vizquel. "Lofton at first, Diaz at second, Cordero at third, fans on their feet. Listen to the crowd… those that remain! The payoff pitch, a swing, and a groundball towards first, down the right field line into the corner. Here comes Cordero, here comes Diaz, here comes Lofton. Unbelievable, unbelievable!"[29] Tom Hamilton The game was tied at 14-14, the Indians scored five-runs in the bottom of the 9th all with 2 outs.

The Mariners kept the score tied going into the bottom of the 11th, 14-14 as Lofton batted with one out. Lofton lined a single into centerfield for his fourth hit of the game. Omar Vizquel advanced Lofton the winning run to second with a single and now it was up to Jolbert Cabrera. "Cabrera…the pitch, swung on, line drive base hit to left, Lofton around third he's goanna score the game winner. McLemore's throw the slide, not in time! The Indians with one of the most stunning comebacks in history! Lofton being carried off the field, and now about to be mobbed is Jolbert Cabrera. The Indians done and buried down twelve in the seventh have completed the miracle! We said in the ninth it may take divine intervention; there will be a lot of people wondering!"[30] Tom Hamilton

JACOBS FIELD
CLEVELAND, OHIO

AS FOR THE Fans, it is important to point out that before, during and after the amazing 455 consecutive game sellout streak there were few fans as loyal as John Adams. The number one Tribe fan John Adams has been attending Indians games with a rally drum since August 24, 1973. At the old Cleveland Municipal Stadium, fans would bang on the seats to make noise since there were hardly any spectators. Prior to one game, John Adams called the ballpark and received permission to bring his rally drum to the game to bang on it. He did not expect it to become a game after game tradition, but it did. John Adams has attended nearly 3,600 games in 45 years, missing less than 50 games in that span. John has a routine of when he bangs on his drum, "I set the roles and so if we have a guy in scoring position that would be second or third. Then I'll start come on let's get him home."[31] When the drumbeat starts Tribe fans all around the ballpark clap to the sound of John's drum. John is one of the nicest guys you will ever meet. I have met John a handful of times and I know I speak for all Cleveland Indian's fans when I say thank you John, keep banging your drum, and GO TRIBE!

Citations

"Cleveland Indians All-Time Roster." *Wikipedia*, Wikimedia Foundation, 8 Oct. 2020, en.wikipedia.org/w/index.php?title= Cleveland_Indians_all-time_roster.

Barnes, Jon. "Bob Lemon." *Society for American Baseball Research*, Admin /Wp-Content/Uploads/2020/02/sabr_logo.Png, 4 Jan. 2012, sabr.org/bioproj/person/bob-lemon/.

Drosendahl, Glenn. *Averill, Howard Earl (1902-1983)*, History Link, 15 Sept. 2010, www.historylink.org/File/9513.

Johnston, *The Seattle Times*, 1974

Getty, United Press, *Everett Daily Herald*, 1929

Lowery, Written by: Cady. "17-Year-Old Bob Feller Makes His First Major League Start." *Baseball Hall of Fame*, 2020, baseballhall.org/ discover/inside-pitch/bob-fellers-starting-debut.

Feller, Robert. "Bob Feller: Gun-Captain to Legendary Pitcher." *Military.com*, 2020, www.military.com/veterans-day/bob-feller.html.

Lemon, Bob. "Bob Lemon Quotes." *BrainyQuote*, Xplore, 2020, www.brainyquote.com/authors/bob-lemon-quotes

IBID.

"42." *"42" Quotes*, Warner Bros. Pictures, 2013, www.quotes.net/movies/42_109688.

Reese, Pee Wee. "Pee Wee Reese Quotations at QuoteTab." *QuoteTab*, 2020, www.quotetab.com/quotes/by-pee-wee-reese.

Rickey, Branch. "Top 30 Quotes of BRANCH RICKEY Famous Quotes and Sayings: Inspringquotes.us." *Inspiring Quotes*, 2020, www.inspiringquotes.us/author/6876-branch-rickey.

McMurray, John. "Larry Doby." *Larry Doby*, Society for American Baseball Research, 2020, sabr.org/bioproj/person/larry-doby/.

IBID.

IBID.

Tom Hamilton; Radio Broadcaster for Cleveland Indians Radio

Jim Thome Delivers Speech after Cleveland Indians Retire His Number, Fox Sports Ohio, 18 Aug. 2018, www.youtube.com/watch?v=uCxFxaYCq-U&t=6s.

Rant, Crypto. *Tom Hamilton's Radio Call of Rajai Davis' World Series Homerun 2016*, YouTube, 27 Mar. 2017, www.youtube.com/watch?v=ZQq0a-AjSu0.

Tom Hamilton's Game-Ending Calls from the 20th, 21st and 22nd Consecutive Victories, Cleveland Indians, 15 Sept. 2017, www.youtube.com/watch?v=BeNTyMRbTmU.

Vizquel Walks off with Grand Slam in 1999, Major League Baseball, 23 May 1999, www.youtube.com/watch?v=AJk0Ty-eGSE.

Indians Improbable Return - Tom Hamilton & Mike Hegan, JLTrain233, 17 May 2014, www.youtube.com/watch?v=8TpSxheQ6QE.

Jim Thome - Longest HR In Cleveland Indians History - Tom Hamilton, JLTrain233, 25 Feb. 2013, www.youtube.com/watch?v=J1aS5ZBq4Xo.

8-20 Indians Walk Off, JLTrain233, 20 Aug. 2016, www.youtube.com/watch?v=q9cIk253cYI.

Tom Hamilton; Radio Broadcaster for Cleveland Indians Radio

5-21 | Indians Win on a Balk! - Tom Hamilton, 21 May 2014, www.youtube.com/watch?v=llOWCGy5GD8.

Tom Hamilton; Radio Broadcaster for Cleveland Indians Radio

IBID.

IBID.

IBID.

IBID.

IBID.

Legendary Cleveland Indians Drummer Tells His Story, Major League Baseball, 7 May 2019, www.youtube.com/watch?v=pe-gjxRi1gU.

About the Author

AUTHOR NICHOLAS BRIGEMAN was born in Akron, OH, in 1992 and grew up in a small town near Cleveland. He is an avid supporter of all Cleveland sports teams and has taken particular interest in baseball and the Cleveland Indians from a young age. Nicholas is currently a Tribe season ticket holder and attends as many games as possible, though he enjoys listening to Tom Hamilton calls the games he can not attend.

Nicholas has also published "Twenty-Two Games of Fame" – A Chronicle of the 2017 Cleveland Indians Win Streak. He has also appeared on local television stations and as an author at the Indian's annual "Tribe Fest" which kicks of each new Tribe season.

CPSIA information can be obtained
at www.ICGtesting.com
Printed in the USA
BVHW070209070121
596801BV00002B/9